So You Think You Know
Indiana University Football

(We'll see about that)

TERRY HUTCHENS

Terry Hutchens Publications

Indianapolis, IN

So You Think You Know Indiana University Football © 2016 Terry Hutchens
ISBN-13: 978-0-9973965-0-8

Cover designed by Phil Velikan.

All interior and cover photos in this book appear courtesy of either the Indiana University Archives, Indiana University Athletics or Indiana University athletics photographer Mike Dickbernd.

Packaged by Wish Publishing

Printed in the United States of America
10 9 8 7 6 5 4 3 2 1

Distributed in the United States by Cardinal Publishers Group.
www.cardinalpub.com

To the powers that be at CNHI Newspaper group for giving me a shot to do what I do best again — work as a beat writer for daily newspapers.

and

To my wife, Susan, for standing beside me and supporting me in my various travels through my life as a journalist, professor, author and most importantly, husband and father.

TABLE OF CONTENTS

Acknowledgements	vii
Introduction — How the Book Works	ix
Chapter 1 — The Warm Up	1
Chapter 2 — Player Trivia	23
Chapter 3 — Coaching Trivia	49
Chapter 4 — Fun Facts Trivia	75
Chapter 5 — Hoosiers in the Pros Trivia	101
Chapter 6 — 1967 Football Trivia	125
Chapter 7 — Venue Trivia	145
Chapter 8 — Who Wore that Number?	171
Chapter 9 — Who am I?	195
Chapter 10 — The Answers	223

ACKNOWLEDGEMENTS

This is my ninth book and the fourth that I have self-published. Three of those have been under the Terry Hutchens Publications umbrella, and one, *Missing Banners*, I co-authored and self-published with Tom Brew. Even in self-publishing, I still have Tom Doherty and Cardinal Publishing handling the distribution. I've had a good relationship with Tom and the Cardinal Publishing family over the years as they have had a role in eight of my nine books.

I want to thank my book handler, Holly Kondras at Wish Publishing, for helping me get through the self-publishing process smoothly again. Our big project this summer was my first children's book, *Hoo-Hoo-Hoo Hoosiers*. Holly helped me produce it along with the incredible illustrations of Phil Velikan. Holly and I have worked together on all of my previous projects, and it's a connection I try not to take for granted. Thanks again, Holly, for your expertise and to Phil for both the children's book and for designing the cover of this trivia book, too.

I wish to thank the IU Archives for giving me permission to use the photographs in this book. Brad Cook was extremely helpful in getting me the images we were able to use for this project.

I want to thank the authors of the various resources I used for this book. The IU Football Media Day that is done annually by Jeff Keag and his staff was the primary resource tool. I also want to thank Ken Bikoff, a long time IU basketball writer and historian. Ken had written a several-part series in Inside Indiana magazine in early 2010 about IU's various athletic venues and the history behind them. I used a great deal of that research in the venue trivia section. I also want to thank Bill Murphy, another excellent IU historian, who helped me with some of the questions regarding the 1967 Rose Bowl team. Bill and I are working on another book together that will be published sometime in 2017.

I also would like to thank a few other people on a personal level. I would like to thank Steve Demas for his inspiration and motivation. Keep fighting the good fight my friend. I'd like to thank the IU Alumni Association and particularly CEO J.T. Forbes and several members of his staff including Mallory Evans, Rachael Jones-McAfee, Michael Mann, Bryan Bradford and Wes Erwin for providing me with opportunities to speak to IU Alumni chapters and tell my stories of 19 seasons covering IU athletics.

Finally, I want to thank my wife, Susan, and my boys, Bryan and Kevin, for their constant support. Whenever I hit that writing wall, Susan is always there to get me pointed in the right direction again.

INTRODUCTION — HOW THE BOOK WORKS

In the summer of 2015, I took a stab at writing an Indiana University basketball trivia book. It was a fun project and well received on different levels. I ended up doing several IU Basketball Trivia nights around the country last year with IU Alumni chapters in places like Orlando, Boynton Beach (Florida), West Lafayette, Louisville, Cincinnati and Bloomington. At several of those stops, I was asked why I didn't have an IU football trivia book? And frankly, I didn't have a good answer. And so I decided this summer I would duplicate the idea and write an Indiana football trivia book.

At one level, this could be considered a highly challenging book of Indiana University football trivia that even the biggest of IU football experts might have a difficult time with the wide variety of questions. On the other hand, you may just be up for the challenge, too. The book is broken up into nine different chapters with various categories of trivia.

At another level, more than just a trivia challenge, this book could serve as a tremendous educational tool that takes you on a trip down memory lane, helping you to relieve some of the great memories from all of IU's greatest players. If you're old enough to remember the 1967 Rose Bowl team for example, there's a chapter just for you to test your skills. Have a good feel for IU coaching greats? There's a coaches trivia chapter, too. Are you one of those IU fans who prides themselves on knowing the uniform numbers worn by various IU standouts over the years? There's a chapter that deals just with player numbers. Are you one of those people who if given a clue about the identity of a certain person can show off your recall and remember that individual? Then the Who Am I? chapter is the one for you. There are 50 biographies there with five clues in each. The challenge is to see how many clues it takes you to guess the identity of the player.

The book begins with a 50-question warm up/general trivia chapter that deals with several topics and gives you the opportunity to gain some early confidence. Next comes player, coach and fun facts trivia which is a hodgepodge of stories and anecdotes from IU football. Next comes a section about Indiana players who have gone on to play professionally, followed by the 1967 Rose Bowl team trivia section. The seventh chapter is venue trivia, looking at the various places where IU football has called home and then there's a chapter the looks at uniform number trivia and other various numerical trivia questions. The trivia challenge wraps up with the 50 biographies which will jog your memory on countless Hoosier greats. All of the answers can be found at the end of the book so that you don't find the urge to glance down to the end of the page for an answer.

All of the questions in the first eight chapters are worth 5 points. With most you earn either 5 or zero. The biographies at the end are worth 4 points each and you can earn anywhere from 1-4 points depending on how quickly you're able to guess that correct player.

But first here's a question to get you started: What Indiana football coach took the Hoosiers to six bowl games in eight seasons and is the winningest coach in IU history? He coached at IU in the 1980s and 1990s. If you guessed Bill Mallory you're off to a good start.

The entire trivia challenge is worth 1,000 points. Eight of the chapters have 50 questions at 2 points each which accounts for 800 points. The biography chapter at the end has 50 questions at 4 points each for another 200 points.

For the die-hard IU football fan who wants to take the trivia challenge, here are a couple of charts to help you grade your performance. Let's say you just want to take one of the individual challenges and test your knowledge in one of the eight chapters. This would be like if you were playing Trivial Pursuit and were just good in Geography. In this case, perhaps it's player or coach trivia that you want to test your skills with.

Whether you use the book as a trivia challenge or an IU football resource guide, I hope you find it to be an enjoyable trip through more than 100 years of Indiana University Football.

INDIVIDUAL CHAPTER SCORECARD (First eight chapters)	
100-88 points	IU National Champion
87-80 points	IU All-American
79-70 points	IU All-Big Ten
69-60 points	Honorable Mention All-Big Ten
59-50 points	Part-time Starter
49-40 points	Not in the two-deep depth chart
39 points and below	Better luck next time

OVERALL TRIVIA CHALLENGE SCORECARD	
1000-880 points	Player of the Year
879-800 points	Hoosier All-American
799-700 points	IU All-Big Ten
699-600 points	Honorable Mention All-Big Ten
599-500 points	Part-time Starter
499-400 points	Not in the two-deep depth chart
399 points and below	Are you a Purdue Grad?

1

THE WARM UP

1. How many times has Indiana played in the Rose Bowl?

A. 3

B. 2

C. 1

D. IU has never played in the Rose Bowl

2. What year did the Hoosiers first begin playing in the current Memorial Stadium?

A. 1970

B. 1960

C. 1965

D. 1975

E. 1980

3. What was the first bowl game that Indiana ever played in?

A. Rose Bowl

B. Copper Bowl

C. Holiday Bowl

D. Independence Bowl

E. All-American Bowl

4. What was the first bowl game that Indiana ever won?

A. Rose Bowl

B. Copper Bowl

C. Holiday Bowl

D. Independence Bowl

E. All-American Bowl

5. What year did Indiana win its first outright Big Ten football championship?

A. 1940

B. 1945

C. 1947

D. 1953

E. 1967

In 2014, Tevin Coleman became the first running back in IU history to eclipse 2,000 yards in one season. He was a third round draft pick of the Atlanta Falcons in the 2015 NFL Draft. (Indiana University Archives, 02_1129_md)

6. Who was the coach of that first outright Big Ten football title team?

A. Clyde B. Smith

B. Phil Dickens

C. Bo McMillin

D. John Pont

E. Bernie Crimmins

7. How many outright Big Ten championships has Indiana won in football?

A. 1

B. 2

C. 3

D. 4

E. 5 or more

8. What year did Indiana and Purdue first begin playing each other in football?

A. 1887

B. 1891

C. 1901

D. 1906

E. 1921

9. What year was the Old Oaken Bucket introduced to the IU-Purdue football rivalry?

A. 1921

B. 1923

C. 1925

D. 1931

E. 1939

10. What decade did Indiana win an all-time best seven games against Purdue?

A. 1990s

B. 1980s

C. 1970s

D. 1950s

E. 1940s

11. What decade did Indiana not win a single game in the IU-Purdue rivalry?

A. 1990s

B. 1980s

C. 1970s

D. 1950s

E. 1940s

12. What rival does Indiana play for the Old Brass Spittoon?

A. Wisconsin

B. Michigan State

C. Michigan

D. Illinois

E. Minnesota

13. What rival did Indiana used to play for the Old Bourbon Barrel?

A. Kentucky

B. Western Kentucky

C. Wabash

D. Louisville

E. Missouri

14. Who is IU's all-time leader in career rushing yards?

A. Anthony Thompson

B. Tevin Coleman

C. Antwaan Randle El

D. Alex Smith

E. Mike Harkrader

15. Who is IU's all-time single season rushing leader?

A. Anthony Thompson

B. Tevin Coleman

C. Antwaan Randle El

D. Alex Smith

E. Mike Harkrader

16. Indiana's all-time individual leader in total offense has more than 3,000 yards more than the No. 2 person on the list. Who is the all-time total offense leader at IU?

A. Anthony Thompson

B. Kellen Lewis

C. Antwaan Randle El

D. Ben Chappell

E. Steve Bradley

17. How many Indiana running backs have eclipsed 1,500 yards rushing in one season in their career?

A. 1

B. 2

C. 3

D. 4

E. 5 or more

18. What is Indiana's longest winning streak in history in the current Memorial Stadium?

A. 6

B. 8

C. 10

D. 12

E. 15

19. Going into the 2016 season, what was the last season where Indiana was ranked in the Associated Press rankings?

A. 2002

B. 1994

C. 1993

D. 1989

E. 1967

20. What Indiana player once returned three kicks of touchdowns? Hint: The year was 2006.

A. Lance Bennett

B. Tandon Doss

C. Ray Fisher

D. James Bailey

E. Marcus Thigpen

21. Indiana's record for most rushing yards in a game by a player is 377 yards in a Big Ten game against Wisconsin. What player ran for 377 yards in one game for the Hoosiers?

A. Anthony Thompson

B. Tevin Coleman

C. Levron Williams

D. Antwaan Randle El

E. Alex Smith

Anthony Thompson was a punishing runner who holds the Indiana career record for rushing yards. He finished second in the Heisman Trophy balloting his senior season. (Indiana University Archives, P0049903)

22. How many times has an Indiana football player ran for more than 300 yards in a game?

A. 1

B. 2

C. 3

D. 4

E. 5 or more

23. How many IU football players have been inducted into the College Football Hall of Fame?

A. 2

B. 3

C. 4

D. 5

E. 7

24. How many IU football coaches have been inducted into the College Football Hall of Fame?

A. 0

B. 1

C. 2

D. 3

E. 4

25. How many former IU football coaches or players have been inducted into the Professional Football Hall of Fame in Canton, Ohio?

A. 10

B. 7

C. 5

D. 3

E. 1

26. How many IU coaches have served as either the head coach or assistant coach in the East-West Shrine Game while they were coaching at IU?

A. 5

B. 4

C. 3

D. 2

E. 1

27. Two of those coaches has been named both an assistant and a head coach in the East-West Shrine Game. Who are those coaches?

A. Lee Corso

B. Bill Mallory

C. Cam Cameron

D. Bernie Crimmins

E. John Pont

28. Where was the 1979 Holiday Bowl played?

A. Los Angeles, California

B. Tempe, Arizona

C. San Diego, California

D. San Antonio, Texas

E. Las Vegas, Nevada

29. Where was the 1986 All-American Bowl played?

A. Atlanta, Georgia

B. Macon, Georgia

C. Huntsville, Alabama

D. Birmingham, Alabama

E. Memphis, Tennessee

30. Where did they play the 1988 Liberty Bowl? (Memphis, Tenn.)

A. Atlanta, Georgia

B. Philadelphia, Pennsylvania

C. Huntsville, Alabama

D. Birmingham, Alabama

E. Memphis, Tennessee

31. What bowl did Indiana play twice in a four-season span?

A. All-American Bowl

B. Liberty Bowl

C. Peach Bowl

D. Copper Bowl

E. Holiday Bowl

32. What bowl game did Indiana record a shutout in by a 24-0 score? Hint: The year was 1991.

A. All-American Bowl

B. Liberty Bowl

C. Peach Bowl

D. Copper Bowl

E. Holiday Bowl

33. Where was the 1993 Independence Bowl played?

A. Memphis, Tennessee

B. New Orleans, Louisiana

C. Baton Rouge, Louisiana

D. Shreveport, Louisiana

E. Dallas, Texas

34. Where was the 2007 Insight Bowl played?

A. San Diego, California

B. Tempe, Arizona

C. Las Vegas, Nevada

D. Los Angeles, California

E. San Francisco, California

35. The 2015 Pinstripe Bowl was played in New York City. But where?

A. Yankee Stadium

B. Giants Stadium

C. Citi Field, Flushing

D. Ebbets Field

E. None of the above

36. True or False? The 2015 Pinstripe Bowl was a defensive struggle with both teams allowing less than 300 yards of total offense.

A. True

B. False

37. True or False? In the final two games of the 2015 regular season, Indiana won back-to-back road Big Ten games over Maryland and Purdue to get bowl eligible?

A. True

B. False

38. True or False? In those final two games of the 2015 regular season, Indiana scored a combined total of more than 100 points?

A. True

B. False

39. Through the 2015 season, how many times has Indiana beat Penn State in history in Happy Valley?

A. 4

B. 3

C. 2

D. 1

E. IU has never beaten Penn State in State College.

40. Indiana and the University of Southern California have played each other four times including in the Rose Bowl after the 1967 season. What is IU's record against USC?

A. 4-0

B. 3-1

C. 2-2

D. 1-3

E. 0-4

41. Since 1968, through the 2015 football season, how many times has Indiana defeated Michigan in football?

A. 5

B. 4

C. 3

D. 2

E. 1

42. Since 1952, through the 2015 football season, how many times has Indiana defeated Ohio State in football?

A. 8

B. 7

C. 5

D. 3

E. 2

43. How many venues has Indiana called home for football?

A. 1

B. 2

C. 3

D. 4

E. 5

44. Through the 2015 Indiana football season, how many total bowl games has Indiana ever played in?

A. 16

B. 10

C. 9

D. 8

E. 6

45. How many different head coaches have coached IU in those games?

A. 6

B. 5

C. 4

D. 3

E. 2

46. How many of those bowl games were coached by Bill Mallory?

A. 3

B. 4

C. 5

D. 6

E. 7

47. True or False? Indiana is undefeated all-time in football against the University of Oklahoma.

A. True

B. False

48. True or False? Indiana is undefeated all-time in football against the University of Florida.

A. True

B. False

49. True or False? Indiana is undefeated all-time in football against the University of Texas.

A. True

B. False

50. Of these four teams, which one owns a victory in football against Indiana: Earlham, Hanover, Vincennes and Xavier?

A. Earlham

B. Hanover

C. Vincennes

D. Xavier

E. None of the above

Bill Mallory is IU's winningest all-time coach. He is known for taking IU to six bowl games in an eight-season stretch. (Indiana University Archives, P0043690)

2

PLAYER TRIVIA

1. Name the only athlete in Indiana history to have ever been named to major All-American teams in both football and basketball?

A. Marv Huffman

B. Vern Huffman

C. Walt Bellamy

D. Antwaan Randle El

E. Branch McCracken

2. How many Indiana football players have been named first team All-American in two different years?

A. 4

B. 3

C. 2

D. 1

E. It has never been done

3. **True or False, Antwaan Randle El was a first team All-American selection in 2001?**

   A. True

   B. False

4. **This IU player was the first in NCAA Division I-A history to pass for 40 touchdowns and score 40 or more non-passing touchdowns?**

   A. Kellen Lewis

   B. Trent Green

   C. Dave Schnell

   D. Antwaan Randle El

   E. Harry Gonso

5. **This player holds the IU record with receiving touchdowns in a season when he caught 16 in 2007?**

   A. James Hardy

   B. Damarlo Belcher

   C. Tandon Doss

   D. Cody Latimer

   E. Courtney Roby

6. **How many IU players have ever been named the Big Ten's most valuable player in football?**

   A. 1

   B. 3

   C. 5

   D. 7

   E. 10 or more

7. **Who holds Indiana's individual record for most yards of total offense in a game? Hint: He put up 475 yards against Michigan.**

   A. Antwaan Randle El

   B. Anthony Thompson

   C. Kellen Lewis

   D. Ben Chappell

   E. Tevin Coleman

8. **In this players' first college game, he had 467 yards of total offense. He threw for 385 yards and ran for 82. Name the player?**

   A. Antwaan Randle El

   B. Kellen Lewis

   C. Ben Chappell

   D. Harry Gonso

   E. Trent Green

9. **What IU player holds the record for most total offense yards in one season with 3,779?**

   A. Antwaan Randle El

   B. Kellen Lewis

   C. Ben Chappell

   D. Harry Gonso

   E. Trent Green

10. **What player had the most career rushing attempts with 1,161 in his IU career?**

    A. Anthony Thompson

    B. Tevin Coleman

    C. Antwaan Randle El

    D. Alex Smith

    E. Vaughn Dunbar

11. Anthony Thompson once ran the ball 47 times in one game against Iowa. But that wasn't the school record that he also holds in a game against Wisconsin. How many carries did A.T. have that day?

A. 48

B. 49

C. 50

D. 51

E. 52

12. In 1998, redshirt freshman Antwaan Randle El was named the opening day starter in a battle against the incumbent starter that went down to the last 24 hours before a decision was made. Who did Randle El beat out to start in 1998?

A. Tommy Jones

B. Blake Powers

C. Earl Haniford

D. Jay Rodgers

E. None of the above

13. In 2001, IU head coach Cam Cameron experimented in the season opener by doing what with Antwaan Randle El?

A. He moved him to running back

B. He moved him to wide receiver

C. He moved him to safety

D. He benched him in favor of another quarterback

E. None of the above

14. How many games did that experiment last?

A. The whole season

B. 5 games

C. 3 games

D. 2 games

E. 1 game

15. Who did the Hoosiers face in that 2001 season opener?

A. North Carolina

B. Clemson

C. Kentucky

D. North Carolina State

E. Oregon

Vaughn Dunbar only played two seasons in Bloomington but gained over 3,000 yards rushing. His sophomore season in 1991 he ran for 1,805 yards and 12 touchdowns. (Indiana University Archives, P0020929)

16. Who started at quarterback in the opener in 2001?

A. Blake Powers

B. Antwaan Randle El

C. Tommy Jones

D. Earl Haniford

E. None of the above

17. The school record for most yards passing in a single game is 480. Who holds the record?

A. Trent Green

B. Dave Schnell

C. Harry Gonso

D. Ben Chappell

E. Nate Sudfeld

18. True or False, in the final two regular season games and the bowl game in 2015, Nate Sudfeld threw for more than 1,000 yards.

A. True

B. False

19. What Indiana quarterback holds the school record for most passing yards in one season with 3,573?

A. Ben Chappell

B. Nate Sudfeld

C. Kellen Lewis

D. Trent Green

E. Dave Schnell

20. Only one time in Indiana history have two running backs eclipsed the 1,000 yard rushing plateau. What year did that occur?

A. 1989

B. 1994

C. 2001

D. 2002

E. 2015

21. Through the 2015 season, how many IU receivers have more than 1,000 yards receiving in a single season in their careers?

A. 1

B. 3

C. 5

D. 6

E. 9

22. The most catches by an IU receiver in one game was 16 and it came in the Old Oaken Bucket game in 1997. Name the player?

A. Chris Gall

B. Duane Gunn

C. Jason Spear

D. Tyrone Browning

E. Versie Gaddis

23. What placekicker holds the IU school record for most field goals in one season with 24?

A. Griffin Oakes

B. Mitch Ewald

C. Scott Bonnell

D. Pete Stoyanovich

E. Austin Starr

24. The school record for tackles in a career is 444, which is 60 more than second place. The player played at IU from 1975-78. Name him.

A. Donnie Thomas

B. Craig Walls

C. Mike Fulk

D. Joe Norman

E. Steve Sanders

25. The school record holder for most tackles also has the record for most tackles in one game. How many did he have?

A. 17

B. 19

C. 24

D. 25

E. 26

26. The school record holder for sacks in a career had at least eight in each of his four seasons at IU. His total was 34.5. The No. 2 person on that list had 25. Name the all-time leader?

A. Adewale Ogunleye

B. Van Waiters

C. Jammie Kirlew

D. Greg Middleton

E. Victor Adeyanju

27. This player had 19 career interceptions, including 14 his first two seasons at IU. He played for the Hoosiers from 1978-82. Name the player?

A. Dave Abrams

B. Chuck Alexander

C. Tim Wilbur

D. Marc Longshore

E. Mark Sutor

28. The school record for the longest interception return was 99 yards set in the Old Oaken Bucket game in 1990. Who has the record?

A. Tim Wilbur

B. Mike Dumas

C. Mark Hagan

D. David Ane

E. Troy Mason

29. This Indiana tailback ran for 227 yards and one touchdown in the 2015 Pinstripe Bowl. Name the player?

A. Jordan Howard

B. Devine Redding

C. Nate Sudfeld

D. Mike Majette

E. Alex Rodriguez

30. Indiana has had two players in history be named two-time Academic All-Americans. Can you name the two players? Hint: One was 2005-06 and the other 1994-95.

A. Austin Starr

B. Graeme McFarland

C. Will Meyers

D. John Hammerstein

E. Brett Law

George Taliaferro was a three-time All-American at Indiana. He may be best known as the first African-American to be drafted by a professional football team. (Indiana University Archives, P0027196)

31. This Indiana player was named All-American three years. Twice he was second team and once he was first team. Can you name the player?

A. Anthony Thompson

B. Antwaan Randle El

C. John Isenbarger

D. Bill Hillenbrand

E. George Taliaferro

32. Only one IU player has ever been named the Big Ten's Most Valuable Player twice. Who is that player?

A. Anthony Thompson

B. Antwaan Randle El

C. John Isenbarger

D. Bill Hillenbrand

E. George Taliaferro

33. This player won the Big Ten MVP in 1979 after leading IU to the Holiday Bowl under Lee Corso. Name the player?

A. Mike Harkrader

B. Lonnie Johnson

C. Tim Clifford

D. Bob Stephenson

E. Tim Wilbur

34. Only two IU players have thrown for 300 yards or more nine or more times in their IU careers. The next closest has accomplished the feat four times. Who are the two players?

A. Ben Chappell

B. Antwaan Randle El

C. Kellen Lewis

D. Nate Sudfeld

E. Trent Green

35. This player returned a punt 62 yards for a touchdown in the fourth quarter to give Indiana a come-from-behind 38-37 win over BYU in the 1979 Holiday Bowl. Can you name the player?

A. John Roggeman

B. Keith Calvin

C. Tim Wilbur

D. Chris Sigler

E. Tony Buford

36. In the 2015 Pinstripe Bowl, this IU receiver caught six passes for 121 yards. Name the player?

A. Ricky Jones

B. Simmie Cobbs Jr.

C. Mitchell Paige

D. Devine Redding

E. Anthony Corsaro

37. In the 2007 Insight Bowl, this IU quarterback ran for 83 yards and a touchdown and threw for 204 yards and two touchdowns. Name the player?

A. Ben Chappell

B. Kellen Lewis

C. Antwaan Randle El

D. Blake Powers

E. Gibran Hamdan

38. In the 1990 Peach Bowl, this IU player scored a pair of touchdowns in the fourth quarter to give IU a 23-20 lead over Auburn before the Tigers came back to score a late touchdown and win. Who scored the two rushing touchdowns from 11 and 2 yards out?

A. Anthony Thompson

B. Vaughn Dunbar

C. Brett Law

D. Trent Green

E. Rob Turner

39. In the 1991 Copper Bowl, this Indiana running back ran for 106 yards and a touchdown in the Hoosiers' win. Who was the running back?

A. Vaughn Dunbar

B. Brett Law

C. Jermaine Chaney

D. Alex Smith

E. De'Wayne Hogan

40. Also in the 1991 Copper Bowl, the same player that scored two fourth quarter touchdowns (and three in all) in the 1990 Peach Bowl had two more rushing scores in this game. Who was the touchdown maker for IU?

A. Anthony Thompson

B. Vaughn Dunbar

C. Brett Law

D. Trent Green

E. Rob Turner

41. Who was the defensive MVP for IU in its shutout performance in the 1991 Copper Bowl?

A. Greg Farrall

B. Lamar Mills

C. Damon Watts

D. Mark Hagan

E. Hurvin McCormick

42. This Indiana player, in the 1991 Copper Bowl, recovered a third quarter fumble in the end zone that thwarted a scoring drive. Who was the player?

A. Greg Farrall

B. Lamar Mills

C. Damon Watts

D. Mark Hagan

E. Hurvin McCormick

43. What IU defensive player earned defensive Most Valuable Player honors for IU in the 1990 Peach Bowl? Hint: He was a free safety who had 14 tackles and four passes broken up.

A. Greg Farrall

B. Mike Dumas

C. Mark Hagan

D. Damon Watts

E. Hurvin McCormick

44. This IU player had six catches for 177 yards and two touchdowns for Indiana in the 1993 Independence Bowl. Name the player?

A. Thomas Lewis

B. Jermaine Chaney

C. Alex Smith

D. Eddie Baety

E. Sean Glover

45. Who was the Indiana starting quarterback in the 1993 Independence Bowl?

A. Chris Dittoe

B. Trent Green

C. John Paci

D. Jay Rodgers

E. Earl Haniford

46. Who was the unlikely recipient of a first down reception in the third quarter of the 2007 Insight Bowl. The reception came on a fourth-and-8 conversion off of a fake field goal attempt?

A. Kellen Lewis

B. Rodger Saffold

C. Charlie Emerson

D. Austin Starr

E. Tracy Porter

47. In another big fake field goal play from the 1988 Peach Bowl, IU scored on a 12 yard fake field run to give the Hoosiers a 22-21 lead in the fourth quarter. What player scored the touchdown for the Hoosiers?

A. Dave Schnell

B. Rob Turner

C. Tim Jorden

D. Anthony Thompson

E. None of the above

48. What IU player was recognized as the defensive most valuable player in the 1988 Peach Bowl? Hint: He played outside linebacker.

A. Willie Bates

B. Van Waiters

C. Mark Hagan

D. Mike Dumas

E. Alfonzo Thurman

49. Who was IU's starting quarterback in the 1988 Peach Bowl?

A. Dave Gramme

B. Trent Green

C. Dave Schnell

D. Earl Haniford

E. Steve Bradley

50. In the 1988 Peach Bowl, this IU wide receiver finished with 246 all-purpose yards. He had 150 yards receiving, 15 rushing and 81 in kickoff returns. Name the player?

A. Rob Turner

B. Anthony Thompson

C. Ernie Jones

D. Eddie Thomas

E. None of the above

Ben Chappell led IU in passing in 2009 and 2010. As of 2016, he still has more than 10 individual school records. (Indiana University Archives, 02_1003_md)

3

COACHING TRIVIA

1. How many head coaches in IU history have won Big Ten football championships while at Indiana?

A. 5

B. 4

C. 3

D. 2

E. 1

2. Which Indiana football coach has won the most games in his IU career? He won 69 games in 13 seasons.

A. Bill Mallory

B. Bo McMillin

C. Lee Corso

D. James Sheldon

E. James Horne

3. Which IU football coach has the second most wins with 63?

A. Bill Mallory

B. Bo McMillin

C. Lee Corso

D. James Sheldon

E. James Horne

4. How many head football coaches has Indiana had since the beginning of the 1980 season?

A. 3

B. 4

C. 6

D. 8

E. 9

5. Billy Herod was IU's third head football coach and coached the Hoosiers in the 1891 season. His record was 1-5 but he claimed the first victory in IU football history. What team did the Hoosiers beat for their first win in history?

A. Butler

B. Louisville Athletic Club

C. Wabash

D. Purdue

E. DePauw

6. Which former IU assistant football coach in 1948 succeeded his boss to become head football coach himself at IU?

A. Bernie Crimmins

B. Clyde Smith

C. Bill Hayes

D. Harlan Page

E. Ewald Stiehm

7. What school did Lee Corso lead to a pair of Missouri Valley Conference titles in four years before become Indiana's head coach in 1973?

A. Duke

B. South Carolina

C. Kentucky

D. Louisville

E. Missouri

8. How many bowl games did IU play in under Corso?

A. 4

B. 3

C. 2

D. 1

E. 0

9. Who was the legendary IU track and field coach who also was the head coach of the Indiana football team from 1931-33? He was 8-14-4 in football but won eight Big Ten titles in track and field.

A. William Ingram

B. Billy Hayes

C. Harlan Page

D. Ewald Stiehm

E. Clarence Childs

10. Which of the following IU coaches DID NOT win the Old Oaken Bucket game in his final season as the Indiana coach?

A. Lee Corso

B. John Pont

C. Bill Mallory

D. Cam Cameron

E. Bo McMillin

Bo McMillin, who coached IU from 1934-47, proudly holds the Old Oaken Bucket. He had a record of 9-4-1 against Purdue in his Indiana career. (Indiana University Archives, P0050816)

11. What was the name of the poem that became Terry Hoeppner's mantra?

A. Play 13

B. Don't Quit

C. Never Ever Quit

D. Have A Plan

E. No Job Is Too Small

12. Who is the only coach in IU football history to ever lead the Hoosiers to an outright Big Ten football championship?

A. Bill Mallory

B. John Pont

C. Lee Corso

D. Sam Wyche

E. Bo McMillin

13. Which of the following coaches did not win his first game his first season as the head coach at Indiana?

A. Bill Mallory

B. Lee Corso

C. Cam Cameron

D. Kevin Wilson

E. All of the above

14. This Indiana football coach's team scored 55 points in his first game ever as the IU coach in a 55-7 win over Indiana State. Who was the coach?

A. Cam Cameron

B. Gerry DiNardo

C. Bill Lynch

D. Terry Hoeppner

E. Kevin Wilson

15. How many head coaches in IU football history have won at least 10 Big Ten games?

A. 8

B. 5

C. 3

D. 2

E. 1

16. Bo McMillin was Indiana's coach from 1934-47. How many winning seasons did IU have in McMillin's 14 seasons with the Hoosiers?

A. 12

B. 10

C. 8

D. 7

E. 6

17. Which former IU head coach served under legendary head coach Frank Leahy at Notre Dame before taking the Indiana job?

A. Bernie Crimmins

B. Clyde Smith

C. Bob Hicks

D. Phil Dickens

E. None of the above

18. In 14 seasons at IU, how many times did Bo McMillin take home the Old Oaken Bucket with a victory over the Boilermakers?

A. 3

B. 6

C. 9

D. 12

E. 13

19. In 1957, IU coach Phil Dickens sat out a season for alleged recruiting violations. Who was IU's coach on an interim basis for the 1957 season?

A. Bernie Crimmins

B. Clyde Smith

C. Bob Hicks

D. John Pont

E. None of the above

20. Prior to coming to Indiana, Phil Dickens had a undefeated season as the head coach at his prior stop in the 1956 season. Where was Dickens before coming to Indiana?

A. Wyoming

B. Montana

C. Idaho

D. Colorado State

E. South Dakota

21. Phil Dickens was a highly-touted running back coming out of college and in fact was a first team All-SEC selection at this school in 1936. What school did Dickens attend?

A. Alabama

B. Florida

C. Auburn

D. Tennessee

E. Ole Miss

22. Which of the following former IU head coaches did not coach at Miami University in Oxford, Ohio?

A. Terry Hoeppner

B. Bill Mallory

C. Sam Wyche

D. John Pont

E. None of the above

23. What former Indiana head football coach is remembered for having a rose in a punch bowl on the podium at his introductory press conference in Bloomington?

A. Terry Hoeppner

B. Gerry DiNardo

C. Cam Cameron

D. Bill Lynch

E. Kevin Wilson

24. This coach was an assistant on Bill Walsh's Super Bowl champion San Francisco 49ers staff following the 1981 season?

A. Lee Corso

B. Sam Wyche

C. Bill Mallory

D. Cam Cameron

E. John Harbaugh

25. How many NFL teams did Sam Wyche serve as head coach for?

A. 4

B. 3

C. 2

D. 1

E. 0

26. Sam Wyche was IU's coach for just one season in 1983 before moving on to coach the Cincinnati Bengals for eight seasons. How many games did IU win in '83?

A. 9

B. 7

C. 6

D. 5

E. 3

27. Which school did Bill Mallory not serve as head coach for?

A. Miami

B. Northern Illinois

C. Colorado

D. Louisville

E. Indiana

28. How many bowl games did Indiana football play under Bill Mallory?

A. 2

B. 3

C. 4

D. 5

E. 6

29. How many bowl games did the Hoosiers win under the tutelage of Bill Mallory?

A. 4

B. 3

C. 2

D. 1

E. 0

Here's a photo of IU coach Bill Mallory early in his Indiana career. (Indiana University Archives, P0049903)

30. Bill Sheldon holds the record for the most wins by an IU coach in his first season at the school. Sheldon accomplished the feat in 1905. How many games did IU win in 1905?

A. 10

B. 9

C. 8

D. 7

E. 6

31. How many games did Bill Mallory win in his first season at Indiana in 1984?

A. 0

B. 2

C. 3

D. 5

E. 7

32. How many seasons did it take Bill Mallory to guide IU to a bowl game?

A. 1

B. 2

C. 3

D. 4

E. 5

33. In a six season span from 1986-91, how many bowl games did Bill Mallory lead IU to?

A. 6

B. 5

C. 4

D. 3

E. 2

34. Bill Mallory's final bowl game was in 1993 when the Hoosiers played in the Independence Bowl. What team did IU face in the Independence Bowl?

A. Baylor

B. Virginia Tech

C. Auburn

D. BYU

E. Stanford

35. What IU head coach coined the phrase "Play 13"?

A. Gerry DiNardo

B. Cam Cameron

C. Bill Mallory

D. Terry Hoeppner

E. None of the above

36. John Pont's final season at Indiana was 1972. Who took Pont's place as the IU head coach?

A. Phil Dickens

B. Lee Corso

C. Bill Mallory

D. Gerry DiNardo

E. Kevin Wilson

37. Who was the first IU alum to serve as head football coach for the Hoosiers?

A. James Sheldon

B. A.B. Woodford

C. Clarence Childs

D. Bernie Crimmins

E. Cam Cameron

38. The second alum to coach Indiana did so more than 100 years after the first? Who was the second one?

A. James Sheldon

B. A.B. Woodford

C. Bill Mallory

D. Bill Lynch

E. Cam Cameron

39. Which Indiana football coach was known for bringing his own oval logo to IU football?

A. Bill Mallory

B. Gerry DiNardo

C. Cam Cameron

D. Terry Hoeppner

E. Kevin Wilson

40. How many seasons did Terry Hoeppner coach football at IU?

A. 6

B. 4

C. 3

D. 2

E. 1

41. Who was the IU athletic director who hired Terry Hoeppner at Indiana?

A. Rick Greenspan

B. Michael McNeely

C. Terry Clapacs

D. Clarence Doninger

E. Fred Glass

42. The season before arriving in Bloomington, Hoeppner led this university to a bowl game out of the Mid-American Conference?

A. Bowling Green

B. Akron

C. Miami

D. Toledo

E. Ball State

43. Who was Hoeppner's quarterback on that team?

A. Tom Brady

B. Peyton Manning

C. Ben Roethlisberger

D. Ryan Leaf

E. Andre Ware

44. When did Terry Hoeppner have his first brain surgery while coach of the Indiana football team?

A. September, 2005

B. November, 2005

C. December, 2005

D. January, 2006

E. February, 2006

45. Indiana opened the 2006 season with two wins and then Terry Hoeppner announced to his players he would have to have a second brain surgery. Three days after the surgery, IU played a home game and Hep went against his doctor's orders and snuck into the suites above the press box to watch the game. Who was the opponent?

A. Nichols State

B. Southern Illinois

C. Northern Illinois

D. Kentucky

E. Michigan State

46. Which of the following were considered Terry Hoeppner's Hep-isms?

A. Have a plan, work the plan, plan for the unexpected

B. We don't have problems, we have opportunities

C. If you think you can or you think you can't you're probably right

D. Don't be soft but don't be stupid

E. All of the above

47. Only one Indiana football coach in history has led the Hoosiers to a bowl game in his first season at the helm. Who was that coach?

A. Bill Mallory

B. Bo McMillin

C. Kevin Wilson

D. John Pont

E. Bill Lynch

48. What bowl did Indiana attend following that coach's first season in Bloomington?

A. Independence

B. All-American

C. Rose

D. Insight

E. Pinstripe

49. How many wins did Kevin Wilson's Indiana football team win in his first season in 2011?

A. 1

B. 2

C. 3

D. 4

E. 5 or more

50. What former IU assistant football coach later went on to be a color commentator on Indiana University football radio broadcasts with play-by-play voice Don Fischer?

A. Al Borges

B. Marty Fine

C. Buck Suhr

D. Danny Thompson

E. Jim Gruden

Terry Hoeppner got his "dream job" when he was hired at Indiana in December of 2004. He only coached at IU for two seasons before passing away from the effects of brain cancer. (Indiana University Archives, P0046979)

4

FUN FACTS TRIVIA

1. **What is the legendary Jim Thorpe's connection to Indiana University?**

   A. He ran track for the Hoosiers

   B. He was a track and field assistant coach at Indiana

   C. He played football at IU

   D. He was an assistant football coach at IU

   E. All of the above

2. **How many years was Thorpe in Bloomington?**

   A. 1 year

   B. 2 years

   C. 3 years

   D. 4 years

   E. 5 or more years

3. This professional golfer has a father who played football at IU and was a fifth round draft pick of Philadelphia in 1967?

A. Phil Mickelson

B. Fuzzy Zoeller

C. Bo Van Pelt

D. Tom Watson

E. Jeff Overton

4. What feat did the 1910 Indiana University football team accomplish that will very well be a record that is never equaled?

A. They weren't scored on the entire season

B. They didn't allow a touchdown the entire season

C. They did not allow an opponent to gain more than 100 yards of total offense in any game

D. They averaged more than 50 points per game

E. All of the above

5. Did that 1910 team finish the season undefeated?

A. Yes

B. No

6. Indiana played two bowl games in the same calendar year. What was the year?

A. 1986

B. 1987

C. 1988

D. 1989

E. 1991

7. From 1994-2016, how many games did IU play in the month of December?

A. 1

B. 2

C. 3

D. 4

E. None of the above

8. Which of the following IU football players DID NOT also play at least one season of basketball at IU?

A. Antwaan Randle El

B. Cam Cameron

C. Isaiah Roundtree

D. James Hardy

E. None of the above

9. For four years at IU, Antwaan Randle El was arguably the most exciting player in the game. What is the single most disappointing aspect of Antwaan Randle El's four-year career at Indiana University?

A. He never had a 350 yard total offense game

B. He didn't throw for more than 7,000 career passing yards

C. He didn't run for more than 3,000 yards in his career

D. He never played in a bowl game at IU

E. All of the above

Anyone that saw Antwaan Randle El play football at Indiana is of the belief that at the time he played he was the most exciting player in college football. (Indiana University Archives, P0021646)

10. What member of the Harbaugh family has a link to Indiana University football?

A. Jim Harbaugh

B. John Harbaugh

C. Jack Harbaugh

D. Joanie Crean

E. None of the above

11. Clarence Childs coached Indiana football in 1914 and 1915. What did he do in 1912 that earned him notoriety in track and field?

A. He won a gold medal in the pole vault in the Olympics in Stockholm

B. He won a silver medal in the shot put in the Olympics in Stockholm

C. He won a bronze medal in the hammer throw in the Olympics in Stockholm

D. He made it to the Olympics but did not receive a medal

E. None of the above

12. In 1931, Indiana and Illinois played to a scoreless tie. The game, however, was awarded to Indiana based on this statistical advantage. What statistic was used to determine the tie-breaker?

A. Total yards

B. First downs

C. Third down conversions

D. Rushing yards

E. Passing yards

13. In 1957, John Meegan was Indiana's leading rusher for the season. How many yards did he gain?

A. 514

B. 414

C. 314

D. 214

E. 114

14. Who was the first IU quarterback to throw for more than 1,000 yards in a season?

A. Bob Hoernschemeyer

B. Nick Sebek

C. Lou D'Achille

D. Kirk Jenkins

E. Steve Sears

15. Who was the first IU receiver to catch more than 1,000 yards in a season? Hint: He had 1,265 receiving yards and 13 touchdowns and he played for Bill Mallory.

A. Thomas Lewis

B. Ernie Jones

C. Mark Ping

D. Duane Gunn

E. Kenny Allen

16. Who was the first IU running back to gain more than 1,000 rushing yards in a season? Hint: He had 1,217 and played his home games in the current Memorial Stadium.

A. John Isenbarger

B. Courtney Snyder

C. Mike Harkrader

D. Lonnie Johnson

E. Anthony Thompson

17. Who was the first IU running back to run for more than 200 yards in a game? Hint: Later that school year, the Indiana basketball team was an undefeated national champion.

A. Mike Harkrader

B. Ric Enis

C. Courtney Snyder

D. Dave Carter

E. Dave Lubovich

18. Who was the first IU quarterback to throw for more than 350 yards in a game? Hint: It happened in the 1980s.

A. Tim Clifford

B. Babe Laufenberg

C. Steve Bradley

D. Dave Kramme

E. Dave Schnell

19. Who was the first IU receiver to go over 200 receiving yards in a game? Hint: His head coach was Lee Corso.

A. Nate Lundy

B. Bob Stephenson

C. Mike Friede

D. Dave Frey

E. Keith Calvin

20. Who was the first IU defensive player to record at least 10 sacks in one season? Hint: He had 14 that season and his team played in the All-American Bowl.

A. Steven May

B. Vincent Fisher

C. Van Waiters

D. Kevin Wyatt

E. Kevin Mulholland

21. Who was the IU quarterback in 2003 and 2004 that transferred to the Hoosiers from Notre Dame?

A. Gibran Hamdan

B. Chris Smith

C. Matt Lovecchio

D. Blake Powers

E. Tim Mullen

22. What member of the Indiana athletics administration and a former IU player and assistant coach had a father who was inducted into the IU Athletics Hall of Fame and was a member of the 1945 outright Big Ten championship football team?

A. Fred Glass

B. Scott Dolson

C. Brad Bomba

D. Mark Deal

E. Chuck Crabb

23. True or False? With travel restrictions in place due to World War II, the Cincinnati Reds and Indianapolis Indians both held spring training in Bloomington from 1943-45.

A. True

B. False

24. True or False? The New York Yankees and baseball star Babe Ruth played an exhibition game in Bloomington in 1921, a year where he would go on to hit 59 home runs.

A. True

B. False

25. What two traditions of Indiana football are credited to Terry Hoeppner for starting at IU?

A. Names on the back of jerseys

B. The Rock

C. Back Home Again in Indiana played before games

D. The Walk

E. The playing of the William Tell Overture

26. Where did The Rock that has a home in the north end zone of the Memorial Stadium have its origin?

A. Found in a quarry in Shelbyville, Ind.

B. Some of the limestone used to build Memorial Stadium.

C. Found at the site of IU's first football stadium

D. Found in West Lafayette, Ind.

E. Found during excavation of the Hoosier Dome in Indianapolis

This photo is from the "Hep Wants You" campaign that Indiana debuted shortly after Hoeppner was hired as IU's head coach. (Indiana University Archives P0043950)

27. In 1915, poor weather prior to the Purdue game forced the Hoosiers to practice in one of its first unofficial indoor practice facilities. Where was the practice held?

A. At the YMCA

B. At a local park

C. At Gentry Farm

D. In the gravel parking lot of the stadium

E. In the Student Union

28. Besides coaching at Indiana, John Pont, Bill Mallory and Terry Hoeppner are also coached at what MAC school?

A. Ball State

B. Toledo

C. Akron

D. Miami

E. Bowling Green

29. What future Cincinnati Reds baseball star starred as a tight end for the Indiana University football team in the mid-1940's?

A. Frank Robinson

B. Ted Kluszewski

C. Gus Bell

D. Joe Nuxhall

E. Ewell Blackwell

30. Where was that future Reds star first discovered by the scouts of the team?

A. At a burger place

B. In the IU library

C. On the football field

D. Taking batting practice for the IU baseball team

E. At an IU baseball game

31. As a 17-year-old freshman quarterback at Indiana in 1943, what was Bob Hoernschemeyer (pronounced HUNCH-meyer) best known for?

A. He threw six touchdown passes in one game.

B. He ran for five touchdowns in one game.

C. He threw for more than 400 yards in one game

D. He ran for more than 200 yards in one game

E. He ran for a touchdown, threw for a touchdown, returned a kickoff and a punt for a touchdown.

32. True or False? Indiana and Notre Dame have played in football since 1990.

A. True

B. False

33. What was the first athletic team at Indiana? It played its games at University Athletic Field in Seminary Square, an 11-acre plot of land.

A. Football

B. Track and Field

C. Rugby

D. Soccer

E. Baseball

34. What team did Indiana play in its first intercollegiate football game in 1887?

A. Wabash

B. Butler

C. DePauw

D. Purdue

E. Franklin

35. What interesting site served as a backdrop for Jordan Field? It is called "God's Acre" and it's still visible today on the IU campus?

A. Hoosier Hill

B. An old chapel

C. Dunn Cemetery

D. Horse stables

E. None of the above

36. What did the university do to Jordan Field in February of 1908 that provided a new activity for students once the temperatures dropped?

A. Put a tarp over it

B. Turned it into an ice skating rink

C. Put down temporary wood flooring and it became a dancing area

D. Put up a tent where students would congregate for activities

E. All of the above

37. True or False? It was reported in 1945 that Ted Kluszewski once hit a ball at Jordan Field that travelled more than 550 feet before breaking a window at the Men's Gymnasium which is currently part of the HPER on the Bloomington campus.

A. True

B. False

38. What happened in the 1987 IU football season that had never happened before and has never happened since?

A. IU went undefeated in Big Ten play

B. IU did not allow a touchdown in Big Ten play

C. IU gave up 50 points in back-to-back games

D. IU scored 50 points in back-to-back games

E. IU defeated both Michigan and Ohio State in the same season

39. True or False? An IU placekicker has earned All-American status at Indiana.

A. True

B. False

40. What is the most number of weeks that Indiana has ever appeared in the Associated Press rankings in one season?

A. 8

B. 7

C. 6

D. 5

E. 4

41. How many of those games did it win while being ranked?

A. 8

B. 7

C. 6

D. 5

E. 4

42. What is the highest ranking an Indiana football team has ever achieved?

A. No. 1

B. No. 2

C. No. 3

D. No. 4

E. No. 5

43. When IU dedicated the original Memorial Stadium in 1925, a special train called the Pennsylvania-Monon "Hot Shot Special" was scheduled that would "whisk fans" from Indianapolis to Bloomington for the game. How long was that train ride from Indianapolis to Bloomington?

A. 4 hours

B. 3 hours

C. 2 hours

D. 90 minutes

E. 1 hour

44. On the dedication day, anticipating a huge crowd, IU employed about 30 ushers to help park cars on the golf links, Jordan Field and Indiana Field. It was an all day job. How much were the parking attendants paid that day?

A. $15

B. $10

C. $5

D. $2.50

E. They weren't paid

45. Since 1908, in the season where Indiana and Purdue have played football, how many times has the IU-Purdue game NOT BEEN the final game of the regular season?

A. 0

B. 1

C. 2

D. 3

E. 4 or more

46. What was the first season that Indiana football ever appeared in the national football rankings?

A. 1940

B. 1942

C. 1945

D. 1958

E. 1967

47. True or False? Indiana and Purdue have played ONE football game in history when both were ranked in the Associated Press rankings.

A. True

B. False

48. True or False? In 1885, Indiana is believed to have fielded its first football team but there is no record of that team having a coach.

A. True

B. False

49. True or False? Indiana's first recorded intercollegiate game came in 1887 but IU's first win in football didn't come until the final game of the 1891 season.

A. True

B. False

50. True or False? Longtime IU broadcaster Don Fischer has been on the call of at least one of IU's Big Ten championships in football.

A. True

B. False

Pete Stoyanovich made 47 field goals in four seasons at Indiana. (Indiana University Archives P0021836)

5

HOOSIER IN THE PROS TRIVIA

1. **As of the 2016 NFL Draft, how many Indiana players have ever been drafted in the first round of the NFL Draft.**

   A. 35

   B. 25

   C. 12

   D. 10

   E. 8

2. **How many of those players were drafted in the top 10 picks overall?**

   A. 16

   B. 11

   C. 8

   D. 7

   E. 4

3. True or False, an Indiana football player has selected the No. 1 selection overall in the NFL Draft?

A. True

B. False

4. This player was IU's first All-American quarterback and was later a third round selection, the 27th player picked overall, by the Detroit Lions in the 1937 NFL Draft.

A. Vern Huffman

B. Bill Hillenbrand

C. Ben Raimondi

D. Bob Hoernschemeyer

E. Nick Sebek

5. What team has drafted more IU players than any other NFL team? Hint: As of 2016, it had drafted nine more than the next closest team.

A. Cincinnati

B. Indianapolis

C. Cleveland

D. Arizona

E. San Diego

6. **True or False. The Kansas City Chiefs have never drafted an IU football player?**

   A. True

   B. False

7. **True or False. The Jacksonville Jaguars have never drafted an IU football player?**

   A. True

   B. False

8. **True or False. The New England Patriots have never drafted an IU football player?**

   A. True

   B. False

9. **What round was Anthony Thompson drafted in the 1988 NFL Draft?**

   A. First

   B. Second

   C. Third

   D. Fifth

   E. Seventh

10. What round was Antwaan Randle El drafted in the 2002 NFL Draft? (2nd)

A. First

B. Second

C. Third

D. Fifth

E. Seventh

11. What round was Trent Green drafted in the 1993 NFL Draft?

A. First

B. Second

C. Third

D. Sixth

E. Eighth

12. What round was John Isenbarger drafted in the 1970 NFL Draft?

A. First

B. Second

C. Third

D. Sixth

E. Not drafted

13. What round was QB Harry Gonso drafted in the 1968 NFL Draft?

A. First

B. Second

C. Third

D. Sixth

E. Not drafted

14. What round was Pete Stoyanovich drafted in the 1989 NFL Draft?

A. First

B. Second

C. Fifth

D. Seventh

E. Eighth

15. What round was Pete Pihos drafted in the 1945 NFL Draft?

A. First

B. Fifth

C. 10th

D. 15th

E. 18th

16. What round was Tracy Porter drafted in the 2008 NFL Draft?

A. First

B. Second

C. Third

D. Fifth

E. Eighth

17. What round was Babe Laufenberg drafted in the 1983 NFL Draft?

A. Third

B. Fourth

C. Fifth

D. Sixth

E. Seventh

18. What round was Joe Norman drafted in the 1979 NFL Draft?

A. First

B. Second

C. Third

D. Fourth

E. Fifth

Doug Crusan was one of four All-Americans on the 1967 Rose Bowl team. (Indiana University Archives, P0020856)

19. What round was Cody Latimer drafted in the 2014 NFL Draft?

A. First

B. Second

C. Third

D. Fourth

E. Fifth

20. What round was Ben Raimondi drafted in the 1946 NFL Draft?

A. First

B. Fifth

C. 10th

D. 22nd

E. 26th

21. Trent Green, Gibran Hamdan, Antwaan Randle El and Tracy Porter have all been on the roster of this NFL team?

A. Pittsburgh

B. Washington

C. Carolina

D. New Orleans

E. Philadelphia

22. Joe Norman is the only player in IU history who has ever been drafted by this team as of the 2016 draft?

A. Oakland

B. Jacksonville

C. Seattle

D. Green Bay

E. Miami

23. Trent Green and Jack Hoffman are two IU players who were drafted by this NFL franchise?

A. St. Louis

B. Arizona

C. Los Angeles

D. Seattle

E. San Diego

24. Ernie Jones, Pete Stoyanovich and Anthony Thompson were all on the roster at one time of this NFL franchise?

A. St. Louis

B. Arizona

C. Kansas City

D. New Orleans

E. Dallas

25. This NFL franchise has drafted 10 IU players but none in the last 30 years through the 2016 NFL Draft?

A. Philadelphia

B. Washington

C. New York Giants

D. New York Jets

E. Buffalo

26. Jammie Kirlew and Cody Latimer were both drafted by this NFL franchise?

A. Seattle

B. San Diego

C. Denver

D. Kansas City

E. Minnesota

27. Doug Crusan and Pete Stoyanovich were both drafted by this NFL franchise?

A. Kansas City

B. Denver

C. New York Jets

D. Miami

E. Washington

28. Terry Cole was drafted by this NFL franchise in 1968 and Marv Woodson was a first round draft pick of this franchise in 1964?

A. Cleveland

B. Baltimore

C. Dallas

D. New York Jets

E. Washington

29. Eric Moore was a first round draft pick of this organization in 1988. Six years later, they used a first round selection and picked Thomas Lewis?

A. New York Giants

B. New York Jets

C. Philadelphia

D. Washington

E. Buffalo

30. Vaughn Dunbar was drafted by the New Orleans Saints but name the other NFL team he played for in 1995?

A. Jacksonville

B. Miami

C. Dallas

D. Detroit

E. Green Bay

31. How many teams did Doug Crusan play for in his NFL career that went from 1968-74?

A. 1

B. 2

C. 3

D. 4

E. 5 or more

32. Trent Green played for five NFL teams and played for this organization twice, first in 1999-2000 and later in 2008?

A. Kansas City

B. St. Louis

C. San Diego

D. Washington

E. Miami

33. Antwaan Randle played with two NFL teams. He had two stints with one of them and actually made it to two Super Bowls, going 1-1 in those games. Which team did he play with in the Super Bowl?

A. Pittsburgh

B. Washington

C. Carolina

D. Jacksonville

E. New York Giants

34. George Taliaferro played with five professional teams, beginning with the Los Angeles Dons in 1949. What team did Taliaferro end his career with? (Philadelphia)

A. Los Angeles Dons

B. New York Yankees

C. Philadelphia

D. Baltimore

E. Dallas

35. This former IU two-sport athlete had stints as an assistant coach with four NFL teams including Washington, San Diego, Baltimore and Miami. He was also a college head coach?

A. Dave Waanstadt

B. Curt Mallory

C. Cam Cameron

D. Jim Gruden

E. John Harbaugh

36. Name the IU player who is in both the college and professional football hall of fames?

A. Anthony Thompson

B. Trent Green

C. Antwaan Randle El

D. Pete Pihos

E. Zora Clevenger

37. This player is best known as the first African-American to be drafted to a National Football League team?

A. Melvin Groomes

B. George Taliaferro

C. Cliff Anderson

D. Ollie Matson

E. Buddy Young

38. Eric Stolberg, Gary Gooden and Nolan Harrison are former IU football players who were all drafted by this professional franchise?

A. Los Angeles Ram

B. Oakland

C. San Diego

D. Seattle

E. Kansas City

39. As of the 2016 NFL draft, the only two players from IU ever selected by this team were a pair of 10th rounders, Chris Morris in 1971 and Bob Riley in 1987. What's the franchise?

A. Green Bay

B. Detroit

C. Chicago

D. Minnesota

E. Tennessee

40. Van Waiters in 1988 is one of seven former IU players who were drafted by this franchise. What is the team?

A. Indianapolis

B. Denver

C. Detroit

D. Cincinnati

E. Cleveland

41. This is a franchise with IU connections but that hasn't helped in the draft process. Steve Lee, and most recently Tandon Doss in 2011 are the only two former IU players drafted by this team. Name the team?

A. Cleveland

B. Baltimore Ravens

C. San Diego

D. Denver

E. Carolina

42. In Super Bowl XLIV against Indianapolis, this New Orleans Saints defensive back and former IU football standout intercepted a Peyton Manning pass and returned it 74 yards for a touchdown that sealed his teams' victory. Name the player?

A. Jabari Greer

B. Tracy Porter

C. Roman Harper

D. Darren Sharper

E. Knute Lentz

43. A second round pick by the St. Louis Rams in 2010, this IU offensive lineman won the starting job at left tackle his rookie season and started every game for the Rams. Name the player? (Rodger Saffold)

A. Rodger Saffold

B. Shawn Harper

C. Charles Peal

D. Chris Liwienski

E. Victor Allotey

44. In 1964, this former IU defensive back was drafted in the first round, the eighth pick overall by the Baltimore Colts. He was also drafted in the third round of the AFL Draft by the Denver Broncos. He played six seasons in the NFL for Pittsburgh and New Orleans. Name the player?

A. Wilbert Scott

B. Randy Williams

C. Marv Woodson

D. Nate Ramsey

E. Mike Wasdovich

45. Four IU players have been selected by this team in history. The most recent was Tevin Coleman in the 2015 draft. Name the team?

A. Carolina

B. Jacksonville

C. Buffalo

D. Atlanta

E. Indianapolis

46. This former IU football standout running back played four seasons for the San Francisco 49ers before having a breakout season as a wide receiver with the Hawaiians in the World Football League in 1974. Name the player?

A. Terry Cole

B. John Isenbarger

C. Tom Nowatzke

D. Lonnie Johnson

E. None of the above

47. This former Hoosier was drafted in 1947 by the All-America Conference's New York Yankees to play professional football. He played his college football at both William & Mary and IU. Name the player?

A. John Cannady

B. Ben Raimondi

C. Bob Ravensberg

D. Jim Goodman

E. Jimmy Dewar

Here are four of the skill players off of the 1945 IU football team. Across the back are Melvin Groomes, Ben Raimondi and George Taliaferro. Up front is Pete Pihos. (Indiana University Archives, P0027159)

48. This former IU standout back was originally drafted in the 11th round of the 1947 draft by the New York Giants. He played with the Chicago Hornets, Chicago Rockets and Brooklyn Dodgers before playing his final six seasons with the Detroit Lions.

A. Rex Grossman

B. Pete Pihos

C. Howard Brown

D. Bob Hoernschemeyer

E. Dick Deranek

49. IU's all-time sacks leader played for three NFL teams beginning in 2000: Miami, Chicago and Houston. The bigger challenge is pronouncing his name. Name the player?

A. Adam Replogle

B. Victor Adeyanju

C. Marcus Freelonjuia

D. Adewale Ogunleye

E. Justin Smith

50. Former Bloomington South quarterback Rex Grossman played his college football at Florida and was a first round draft pick of the Chicago Bears in 2003. His grandfather played at IU and played for both the Baltimore Colts and the Detroit Lions from 1948-51. What is his grandfather's name?

A. Gunner

B. Johnnie

C. Ralph

D. Francis

E. Rex

John Isenbarger is shown carrying the ball in the 1967 Rose Bowl game against Southern California. (Indiana University Archives, P0029557)

6

1967 FOOTBALL TRIVIA

1. **The 1967 season was John Pont's third year at Indiana. How many total games did IU win in Pont's first two seasons?**

   A. 8

   B. 4

   C. 3

   D. 2

   E. 1

2. **What was IU's record in 1966, the year before the Rose Bowl season?**

   A. 1-8-1

   B. 2-7-1

   C. 0-10

   D. 6-4

   E. 4-6

3. How many games did IU win in a row to open the 1967 season?

A. 10

B. 9

C. 8

D. 7

E. 6

4. After IU won at Michigan 27-20 on Oct. 20, 1967 it was ranked for the first time that season. What was the ranking?

A. 25th

B. 22nd

C. 15th

D. 10th

E. 6th

5. How many weeks in a row was IU then ranked beginning with the Oct. 28 game at Arizona?

A. 8

B. 6

C. 5

D. 4

E. 3

6. Prior to being ranked in 1967, when was the last time an IU football had been ranked?

A. 1965

B. 1962

C. 1955

D. 1950

E. IU had never been ranked before

7. IU was 9-1 in the regular season in '67. What team handed IU its only regular season loss?

A. Purdue

B. Wisconsin

C. Minnesota

D. Ohio State

E. Michigan

8. What was IU's final Associated Press ranking in 1967?

A. No. 5

B. No. 4

C. No. 3

D. No. 2

E. No. 1

Ken Kaczmarek had a big body and was strong as an ox. He was an All-American in 1967, too. (Indiana University Archives, P0021272)

9. What was Purdue ranked coming into the Old Oaken Bucket game in 1967?

A. No. 10

B. No. 7

C. No. 4

D. No. 3

E. The Boilermakers were not ranked

10. How about IU? Where were the Hoosiers ranked going into the Old Oaken Bucket game in 1967?

A. No. 10

B. No. 7

C. No. 4

D. No. 3

E. The Hoosiers were not ranked

11. IU had one captain on its 1967 Rose Bowl team. Who was the captain?

A. Doug Crusan

B. Harry Gonso

C. John Isenbarger

D. Bob Van Pelt

E. Terry Cole

12. IU was co-Big Ten champs with a 6-1 record. What was the largest margin of victory in any of those six games?

A. 42

B. 3

C. 7

D. 10

E. 13

13. How many ranked teams did IU play during that season including the bowl game?

A. 2

B. 3

C. 4

D. 5

E. 6 or more

14. Prior to beating Purdue in the Old Oaken Bucket game, how many games had IU lost in a row to ranked opponents?

A. 5

B. 11

C. 27

D. 30

E. 35

15. What year had IU previously defeated a ranked opponent?

A. 1963

B. 1960

C. 1958

D. 1954

E. 1945

16. What was the last year IU had defeated a ranked opponent at home?

A. 1950 vs. Iowa

B. 1950 vs. Notre Dame

C. 1949 vs. Pittsburgh

D. 1946 vs. Illinois

E. 1945 vs. Purdue

17. How many games did IU win 1967 by five points or less?

A. 2

B. 3

C. 4

D. 5

E. 6

18. How many games in 1967 did IU score more than 28 points?

A. 1

B. 2

C. 3

D. 4

E. 6 or more

19. Both of USC's touchdowns in the Rose Bowl were scored by this All-American running back?

A. Frank Gifford

B. Jim Brown

C. Walter Payton

D. O.J. Simpson

E. Marcus Allen

20. What was the nickname of the 1967 IU football team?

A. The Clutch Kids

B. The Hurryin' Hoosiers

C. The Cardiac Kids

D. The Fourth Quarter wonders

E. The Rose Bowl Bunch

21. True or Fales. With 110 yards passing the Rose Bowl, Harry Gonso was the game's leading passer?

A. True

B. False

22. What was USC's national ranking going into the Rose Bowl following the 1967 season?

A. No. 1

B. No. 2

C. No. 3

D. No. 5

E. No. 8

23. USC defeated UCLA 21-20 to advance to the Rose Bowl that season. What was UCLA ranked in the nation before it lost to USC?

A. No. 1

B. No. 2

C. No. 3

D. No. 5

E. No. 8

24. The Hoosiers held the Trojans to 14 points in a 14-3 loss. How many other opponents that season held USC to 14 points or less?

A. 4

B. 3

C. 2

D. 1

E. No one had done it all season

25. How many IU players earned All-American status in 1967?

A. 5

B. 4

C. 3

D. 2

E. 1

26. Name the IU wide receiver who as a sophomore in 1967 had 10 touchdown receptions? In fact, he had 10 as a junior and 10 more as a senior, too.

A. Bill Malinchak

B. Bill Couch

C. Jade Butcher

D. Alan Dick

E. John Andrews

27. How many IU players rushed for 100 yards or more in a game in 1967?

A. 0

B. 1

C. 2

D. 3

E. 4

28. This player ran for 155 yards that season in the Old Oaken Bucket victory over Purdue. Name the player.

A. Terry Cole

B. John Isenbarger

C. Harry Gonso

D. Mike Krivoshia

E. None of the above

29. One IU player had three 100-yard rushing games for IU in 1967. Name him.

A. Terry Cole

B. John Isenbarger

C. Harry Gonso

D. Mike Krivoshia

E. None of the above

30. Who was IU's leading rusher in the Rose Bowl? Hint: He had 38 yards on 12 carries.

A. Terry Cole

B. John Isenbarger

C. Harry Gonso

D. Mike Krivoshia

E. None of the above

Harry Gonso was the quarterback for Indiana on the 1967 Rose Bowl team. (Indiana University Archives, P0021040)

31. How many different IU players caught at least one pass in the Rose Bowl game?

A. 6

B. 5

C. 4

D. 3

E. 2

32. True or False. Indiana piled up more than 400 yards of total offense despite scoring just three points in the Rose Bowl game?

A. True

B. False

33. Jade Butcher had seven 100-yard receiving games in his IU career. How many did he have in 1967?

A. 7

B. 6

C. 5

D. 4

E. 3

34. How many total receivers had 100-yard receiving games for IU in 1967?

A. 4

B. 3

C. 2

D. 1

E. 0

35. Harry Gonso had four career passing games with 200 yards or more. How many came in 1967?

A. 4

B. 3

C. 1

D. 1

E. 0

36. True or False. John Pont was the national coach of the year following the 1967 season?

A. True

B. False

37. True or False. John Pont is member of the IU Athletics Hall of Fame?

A. True

B. False

38. True or False. The 1967 season was Doug Crusan's only season playing defense?

A. True

B. False

39. True or False. The 1967 Hoosiers had a player who was both the Big Ten MVP and an All-American selection?

A. True

B. False

40. True or False. Jerry Greco led Indiana in tackles for loss in 1967 with nine.

A. True

B. False

41. True or False. Benjamin Norman had five interceptions for IU in 1967.

A. True

B. False

42. Jade Butcher set school record in this category during the 1967 season that held up until Ernie Jones broke it in 1987.

A. Most receiving yards in a game

B. Most receiving touchdowns in a game

C. Most receiving touchdowns in a season

D. Most receiving touchdowns in a career

E. Most completions in a season by a wide receiver

43. What player scored the most points for Indiana in 1967? His point total was 60.

A. Harry Gonso

B. Terry Cole

C. Jade Butcher

D. John Isenbarger

E. None of the above

44. True or False. When Ken Kaczmarek earned All-American honors at linebacker for the 1967 season, he became the fourth linebacker in the past 10 seasons at IU to earn All-American recognition.

A. True

B. False

45. True or False. When John Isenbarger was named a first team All-American in both 1967 and 1968, he became the first IU player in history to capture first team All-American honors in two different seasons.

A. True

B. False

46. From what town in Ohio, did IU quarterback Harry Gonso hail?

A. Toledo

B. River Falls

C. Findlay

D. Cincinnati

E. Orrville

47. Who was selected as IU's most valuable player in 1967?

A. Harry Gonso

B. John Isenbarger

C. Jade Butcher

D. Doug Crusan

E. Ken Kaczmarek

48. Only two players from the 1967 IU team earned academic All-Big honors in both 1967 and 1968. Gonso was one of them. Who was the other?

A. John Isenbarger

B. Gary Cassells

C. Tom Bilunas

D. Vic Malinovsky

E. Tom Schuette

49. The first name of one of IU's starting linebackers in the Rose Bowl was a color. What was this player's first name?

A. Red

B. Brown

C. Blue

D. Tan

E. Whitey

50. How many IU starters on the Rose Bowl team were named either Harry or Harold?

A. 1

B. 2

C. 3

D. 4

E. 5

7

VENUE TRIVIA

1. **When Indiana football debuted in the mid 1880's, where did the Hoosiers play their home games?**

   A. Bloomington High School

   B. University Athletic Field at IU's Seminary Square

   C. University Athletic Field at Jefferson Park

   D. Monroe Field

   E. Wabash Park

2. It wasn't long before the program outgrew that facility and moved to what was called Jordan Field. What year did the Hoosiers first begin playing at Jordan Field?

A. 1885

B. 1887

C. 1888

D. 1890

E. 1891

3. Who was Jordan Field named for?

A. David Starr Jordan

B. Matthew Robinson Jordan

C. Michael Francis Jordan

D. Thomas Jordan

E. William B. Jordan

4. Who was the opponent in the first game at Jordan Field in 1897? The game finished in a tie at 6-6 and IU would go to win six of its final seven games of the season.

A. Bedford

B. Manual Training

C. DePauw

D. Wabash

E. Rose Polytechnic

5. What was the seating capacity at Jordan Field?

A. 2,500

B. 6,000

C. 8,000

D. 16,555

E. 19,222

Here is an early shot of Jordan Field, early home to the Hoosiers. (Indiana University Archi ves, P0056314)

6. Where on today's campus would Jordan Field have existed?

A. Next to the Sample Gates

B. Fee Lane and the Bypass

C. Behind the IU Auditorium

D. The parking lot next to Assembly Hall

E. The parking lot next to the IU Memorial Union

7. True or False? There is a marker that was placed near where Jordan Field used to stand by the "I" Men's Association although it is somewhat covered by a large bush.

A. True

B. False

8. Indiana moved from Jordan Field to the original Memorial Stadium in time for the 1925 season. In the Bloomington Telephone newspaper, there was a story that announced that the IU-Purdue game that season would be the final game played at Jordan Field and that a new athletic field would be "built soon just north of the present field." What year did that story appear in the newspaper?

A. 1924

B. 1923

C. 1922

D. 1918

E. 1915

9. What initially delayed the construction of the original Memorial Stadium?

A. Lack of funds

B. The field was not deemed to be safe

C. The country was preparing to go to war

D. The Bloomington mayor opposed the idea

E. A fire that destroyed the construction site

10. A few years later, the Indiana University Alumni Association proposed a Memorial Fund that would pay for three major projects including a new football stadium. The other two were give first priority. What were the other two projects?

A. A new women's dormitory

B. A new men's dormitory

C. A new physical education building

D. An auditorium that could also be in the form of a Student Union

E. An on-campus eatery

11. What was the monetary goal for the Memorial Fund that would pay for those three projects?

A. $10,000

B. $50,000

C. $100,000

D. $250,000

E. $400,000

12. In the first meetings when plans for the original Memorial Stadium were proposed, where was the stadium to be constructed?

A. The current site of Ernie Pyle Hall

B. The current site of Mellencamp Pavilion

C. The current site of the DeVault Alumni Center

D. The current site of the Law School

E. The current site of the Fine Arts Museum

13. Later a decision was made to build the original Memorial Stadium on the site of what had been a golf course. What was its location?

A. What is now the IU golf course

B. What is now the IU auditorium

C. What is now Assembly Hall

D. What is now the main library

E. What is now an area that stretches from Woodlawn Avenue to Jordan Avenue

14. When bids were taken to build the original Memorial Stadium they ranged from a high bid of $149,700 to a low bid of $101,250. The board accepted the low bid. Which bid earned the contract?

A. National Concrete Fireproof Co. of Cleveland

B. Bedford Steel and Construction

C. Rice Jones Co. of Cleveland

D. The Blanchard Building Company of Dayton

E. Scott Construction Company of Indianapolis

15. In the spring of 1924, the construction of Memorial Stadium faced another significant setback. What was it?

A. A lumber issue

B. A concrete issue

C. Not enough workers

D. An insurance issue

E. A flooding issue

16. Where did Indiana football play three games during the 1924 season?

A. Hoosier Field

B. Indiana Field

C. Sembower Field

D. The area now known as Bart Kaufman Field

E. Bloomington High School

17. True or False. In September of 1978 the movie "Breaking Away" staged a Little 500 race at the original Memorial Stadium because the IU Student Foundation promised the film maker than 20,000 extras would show up?

A. True

B. False

18. In 1910, Indiana played a neutral site game against Wisconsin in Indianapolis. Where was that game played?

A. Broad Ripple Park

B. Washington Park

C. Garfield Park

D. The area now known as Sahm Golf Course

E. Holiday Park

19. What was a special mode of transport that was offered on the day of the game for fans to get from Bloomington to Indianapolis?

A. Fan busses

B. Fan automobile caravan

C. Trains

D. Planes

E. Boat

20. The first game at Memorial Stadium was played later in the 1924 season on Nov. 15, 1924. IU won the game, 21-7. What school was the opponent that day?

A. Purdue

B. DePauw

C. Wabash

D. Rose Polytechnic

E. Chicago

21. True or False, when Memorial Stadium was officially christened in 1925, IU's Class of '25 provided the university with a gift which was a gate to be placed at the west end of the stadium to serve as an entrance. That gate is still there today.

A. True

B. False

22. What was the final cost of Memorial Stadium, including the cost of demolition and reconstruction of the facility? The original bid remember had been $101,250.

A. $256,487.09

B. $985,241.09

C. $108,250.09

D. $150,000.09

E. $98,235.09

23. What was the capacity of the original Memorial Stadium when it was unveiled in 1925?

A. 15,000

B. 18,000

C. 22,000

D. 28,000

E. 9,800

24. On Nov. 15, 1924, a cornerstone was laid at the southwest end of the stadium and a copper box, a time capsule, was stuffed with mementos from the day. Which of the following items DID NOT find its way into the time capsule?

A. A commencement program from 1924

B. A class schedule of the current semester

C. A course catalog from 1924

D. A copy of the Indiana Daily Student

E. A DVD of the construction progress for the stadium

25. True or False? The stadium was built as a memorial to Indiana athletes who fought in the Civil War.

A. True

B. False

26. A tarp for the original Memorial Stadium field was sewn by W. Wiley and Son. How many yards of surplus Army canvas was used for the tarp?

A. 1,000 yards

B. 10,000 yards

C. 13,000 yards

D. 20,000 yards

E. 23,000 yards

27. Where was that stadium located on campus?

A. On 10th Street where the Arboretum now stands

B. On the current site of Assembly Hall

C. On the current site of Mellencamp Pavilion

D. On the current site of Cook Hall

E. On the current site of Franklin Hall

28. Indiana's first win at Memorial Stadium in 1925 was a 31-0 victory over Indiana State Normal on Oct. 3 in the season opener. The dedication game, however, was played Nov. 21 and it would feature IU and Purdue. Besides being the dedication game, what else was special about that particular game that ended in a 0-0 tie?

A. The first game where teams had face guards on helmets

B. The first game where IU had cheerleaders

C. The debut of the Old Oaken Bucket

D. The first game every covered by the Indiana Daily Student

E. Don Fischer's first game calling Indiana football

29. In 1951, Memorial Stadium was the site of what inaugural event?

A. The North-South High School football game

B. The first Little 500 race

C. A state-wide Boy Scout conference

D. Playing Michigan State for the Old Brass Spittoon

E. All of the above

Here is a shot of Memorial Stadium on 10th Street. (Indiana University Archives, P002

33

30. What was the estimated crowd for that first event?

A. 458

B. 1,222

C. 4,500

D. 5,200

E. 7,000

31. After they stopped running the event or events there, where did it move to?

A. Bill Armstrong Stadium

B. The fields near the Memorial Union

C. The area now known as the IU Golf Course

D. The area now known as Mellencamp Pavilion

E. The area now known as the DeVault Alumni Center

32. What year did the current Memorial Stadium open?

A. 2000

B. 1994

C. 1976

D. 1960

E. 1950

33. When did they break ground for the current Memorial Stadium?

A. Aug. 27, 1998

B. Aug. 27, 1992

C. Aug. 27, 1974

D. Aug. 27, 1958

E. Aug. 27, 1948

34. What was the construction cost of the current Memorial Stadium?

A. $10.2 million

B. $38.45 milion

C. $1.45 million

D. $4.56 million

E. $8.88 million

35. Who was IU's first opponent in the current Memorial Stadium?

A. Oregon

B. Oregon State

C. California

D. Washington

E. Washington State

36. What was IU's first victory in the current Memorial Stadium?

A. Missouri

B. Southern Illinois

C. Western Kentucky

D. Marquette

E. Oklahoma State

37. What was the seating capacity of Memorial Stadium from the time it was built in 1960 thru 1968?

A. 52,929

B. 48,454

C. 46,222

D. 45,200

E. 43,345

38. What is the capacity of Memorial Stadium today?

A. 55,356

B. 56,223

C. 53,112

D. 52,929

E. 48,454

39. The largest crowd ever at Memorial Stadium was 56,223 in 1969. Who was IU's opponent that day?

A. Ohio State

B. Michigan

C. Wisconsin

D. Kentucky

E. Purdue

40. Over the years, Indiana has often taken aerial shots of Memorial Stadium at capacity when a certain opponent comes to Bloomington. What school is known for filling up Memorial Stadium when its team plays in Bloomington?

A. Ohio State

B. Michigan State

C. Wisconsin

D. Kentucky

E. Purdue

41. After Indiana stopped playing in the original Memorial Stadium following the 1959 season, what other IU team or group would call the stadium home?

A. Track and Field

B. Soccer

C. Rugby

D. Marching Hundred

E. All of the above

42. In 1971, the name of the current Memorial Stadium was changed from 17th Street Stadium to Memorial Stadium. What was the original Memorial Stadium then renamed?

A. Third Street Stadium

B. 10th Street Stadium

C. Hoosier Field

D. Indiana Stadium

E. Memorial Field

43. What year did they demolish the original Memorial Stadium?

A. 1990

B. 1982

C. 1974

D. 1970

E. 1963

44. What happened in the current Memorial Stadium in 1967 that had never happened before?

A. Indiana shut out three opponents at home

B. Indiana won all of its home games

C. Indiana beat Michigan State and Michigan in the same season

D. Lights were installed so that night games could be played

E. Ticket Prices were raised to $10 per game

45. Through the 2015 season, the Memorial Stadium record for average attendance was 53,319 in five home games. Interestingly, IU was just 2-3 in those games. What season was the average attendance record set?

A. 2014

B. 2008

C. 1988

D. 1972

E. 1969

46. What was the original playing surface of the current Memorial Stadium?

A. Astroturf

B. Grass

C. Cardboard (because IU always looks better on paper)

47. True or False, IU installed an AstroTurf surface in 1986 but then replaced it with natural grass in 1998.

A. True

B. False

48. True of False. In June of 2008, heavy rains created a sink hole in the south end zone of the current Memorial Stadium.

A. True

B. False

49. What year did construction begin to close the north end zone of Memorial Stadium?

A. 2006

B. 2007

C. 2008

D. 2009

E. 2010

50. In March of 2016, Indiana announced plans to enclose the south end zone of Memorial Stadium, too. When is that project expected to be completed?

A. In time for the 2017 season

B. In time for the 2018 season

C. In time for the 2019 season

D. In time for the 2020 season

E. In time for the 2021 season

Here is a photo of Memorial Stadium while under construction. (Indiana University Archives, P0022473)

8

WHO WORE THAT NUMBER? AND OTHER NUMBERS TRIVIA

1. **They don't officially retire jersey numbers at Indiana but no one has worn this number since Anthony Thompson last wore it for the Hoosiers in 1989. What is the number?**

   A. 32

   B. 33

   C. 25

   D. 28

   E. 35

2. **Antwaan Randle El and Dave Schnell were two of seven former IU quarterbacks that wore this number at Indiana. What number was it?**

   A. 10

   B. 11

   C. 12

   D. 1

   E. 8

3. **Who was the only quarterback in IU history to wear No. 1?**

   A. Scott Arnett

   B. Woody Moore

   C. Byron Broome

   D. Allen Webb

   E. Antwaan Randle El

4. **What number was made famous at IU by Tevin Coleman when he rushed for more than 2,000 yards in 2014?**

   A. 9

   B. 8

   C. 6

   D. 4

   E. 2

5. **Vaughn Dunbar made this number famous at IU. What was the number?**

   A. 24

   B. 25

   C. 26

   D. 27

   E. 28

6. **Twelve quarterbacks wore this number including Chris Dittoe, Tommy Jones, Blake Powers and Tim Clifford. What was the number?**

   A. 11

   B. 12

   C. 13

   D. 10

   E. 14

7. **The great George Taliaferro wore this number. What was it?**

   A. 11

   B. 22

   C. 33

   D. 44

   E. 55

8. Levron Williams wore this number in 2001 when he rushed for 19 touchdowns, including six against Wisconsin. What number did he wear?

A. 8

B. 7

C. 6

D. 5

E. 4

9. Austin Starr's 49-yard field goal in the final minute against Purdue in 2007 sent Indiana to the Insight Bowl in Tempe, Ariz. in the Play 13 season for Terry Hoeppner. What number did Austin Starr wear?

A. 39

B. 36

C. 22

D. 20

E. 18

10. True or False? Rose Bowl starting quarterback Harry Gonso wore No. 12.

A. True

B. False

11. True or False? Trent Green wore No. 12 at Indiana.

A. True

B. False

12. True or False? Pete Stoyanovich wore No. 12 at Indiana.

A. True

B. False

13. True or False? Nate Sudfeld wore No. 9 his freshman season at Indiana.

A. True

B. False

14. True or False? Sudfeld's nemesis at the quarterback spot in the 2013 season, Tre Roberson, wore No. 5 for the Hoosiers.

A. True

B. False

15. True or False? Both Cam Cameron and his son Danny, both wore No. 18 at Indiana.

A. True

B. False

16. True or False? The player that Antwaan Randle El beat out for the quarterback job in the 1998 season wore No. 12.

A. True

B. False

17. Terry Cole and Van Waiters both wore this number at Indiana. What was the number?

A. 48

B. 46

C. 44

D. 43

E. 42

18. True or False? The number 99 has been worn by a kicker, a defensive lineman, defensive back, a linebacker, a tight end and an offensive lineman.

A. True

B. False

19. Pete Pihos wore this number as a tight end at Indiana. James Hardy wore it, too.

A. 88

B. 86

C. 84

D. 82

E. 80

20. True or False? A kicker wore No. 76 at Indiana.

A. True

B. False

21. Both Mike Replogle and Tyler Replogle wore this number. What was the number?

A. 48

B. 46

C. 44

D. 43

E. 42

Bob Ravensburg, John Tavener and John Cannady played together in the early 1940's at IU. (Indiana University Archives, P0045872)

22. Tandon Doss, Versie Gaddis, Marcus Thigpen and T.J. Simmons have all worn this number. What is it?

A. 1

B. 2

C. 3

D. 4

E. 5

23. Mike Dumas, the player who holds the school record for the longest interception return of 99 yards against Purdue, wore this number. What was it?

A. 34

B. 36

C. 38

D. 40

E. 44

24. Josiah Sears, one of the co-captains for the 2007 Indiana football team that played 13 for Terry Hoeppner and played in the Insight Bowl, wore this number. What was it?

A. 48

B. 46

C. 44

D. 43

E. 42

25. Long time IU associate athletic director Harold Mauro wore this number when he was a center on IU's Rose Bowl team in 1967. What was it?

A. 57

B. 55

C. 53

D. 51

E. 50

26. Carl Barzilauskas wore this number first and then later his son Bo Barzilauskas wore it at IU, too. What was the number?

A. 77

B. 78

C. 79

D. 68

E. 69

27. Ted Kluszewski, Kris Dielman and Ted Bolser all wore this number at Indiana. What number?

A. 81

B. 82

C. 83

D. 84

E. 85

28. Which of the following numbers has never been worn by an Indiana football player?

A. 99

B. 98

C. 19

D. 53

E. 0

29. This number was worn by IU's all-time career sacks leader and his last season was 1999. What number was it?

A. 92

B. 93

C. 94

D. 95

E. 96

30. This number is often reserved for an offensive lineman but it was one of two numbers worn by linebacker Ken Kaczmarek, a member of the 1967 Rose Bowl team. The other number he wore was 52. What is the number?

A. 60

B. 61

C. 62

D. 63

E. 64

31. Indiana All-American tackle Jason Spriggs, an Outland Trophy semifinalist, wore this number. His last season was 2015. What was the number?

A. 77

B. 78

C. 79

D. 67

E. 68

32. Joseph Bartkiewicz played at IU from 1946-49, John Bartkiewicz played for the Hoosiers from 1952-55 and Leonard Bartkiewicz played at IU in 1960. A fourth Bartkiewicz, Walter, also played from 1946-49. The first three, though, at one time or another in their IU careers all wore the same number at IU. What was the number?

A. 22

B. 33

C. 44

D. 55

E. 66

33. Numbers 75, 85 and 99 were all numbers worn by this former IU player who went on to be one of IU's strength and conditioning coaches. He played at IU from 1990-92. Who was the player?

A. Stephen Houston

B. Nick Middlebrook

C. Matt Bomba

D. Tom Zupancic

E. Marvin Johnson

34. Bob Kizer isn't a famous IU player from the Mallory era but he's a buddy of mine and a buddy of Dan Dakich's so I thought it would be nice to mention him in my IU football trivia book. He wore two numbers at IU. One of them was 83. What other number did Kizer wear?

A. 86

B. 85

C. 84

D. 82

E. 81

35. Here are a few other "number" trivia questions. What is the "number" of the most penalties ever in a single game by the Indiana football team? Hint: It happened in a victory in one of Kevin Wilson's first games as the IU head coach in 2011.

A. 15

B. 16

C. 17

D. 18

E. 19

36. What is the IU record for the "number" of pass attempts in a game? Hint: Ben Chappell was the quarterback.

A. 70

B. 66

C. 64

D. 62

E. 58

37. What is the "number" of men with the last name of Mallory who have served as either the head coach or an assistant coach of Indiana football?

A. One

B. Two

C. Three

D. Four

E. Five

38. What is the "number" of men with the last name of Mallory who have ever lettered in football at Indiana?

A. 0

B. 1

C. 2

D. 3

E. 4

39. What is the "number" of men with the last name of Lynch that have served as either the head coach or an assistant coach of Indiana football?

A. 1

B. 2

C. 3

D. 4

E. 5

40. Twenty-seven players with this last name have played football at Indiana. What is the last name?

A. Smith

B. Jones

C. Johnson

D. Davis

E. Replogle

41. What last name is second all-time with 24 players having had this last name at IU?

A. Smith

B. Jones

C. Johnson

D. Davis

E. Replogle

42. What is the "number" of players with the last name of Randle El who have played football at Indiana?

A. 1

B. 2

C. 3

D. 4

E. 5

43. What is the "number" of seasons that Indiana has been ranked in the Associated Press football rankings?

A. 4

B. 5

C. 8

D. 11

E. 15

44. When Indiana played its first intercollegiate game in 1897, what was the "number" of players that IU suited up for that game?

A. 43

B. 33

C. 23

D. 15

E. 12

45. What is the "number" of coaches in Indiana football history who have earned Big Ten coach of the year honors?

A. 1

B. 2

C. 3

D. 4

E. 5

46. What is the "number" of players in Indiana football history who have earned Big Ten freshman of the year honors?

A. 0

B. 1

C. 2

D. 3

E. 4

Anthony Thompson is the most famous player to ever wear No. 32 at Indiana. (Indiana University Archives, P0021893)

47. What is the "number" of years that Kevin Wilson's contract was extended in 2016 after the IU football team played in the Pinstripe Bowl in New York City in December of 2015?

A. 2

B. 3

C. 4

D. 5

E. 7

48. What is the "number" of seasons that Indiana has played neutral site games in Indianapolis?

A. 1

B. 2

C. 4

D. 5

E. 7

49. What was the "number" of years that Tenth Street Stadium played host to the Little 500 bike race in Bloomington?

A. 2

B. 8

C. 10

D. 20

E. 30

50. What is the "number" of the street address at Memorial Stadium?

A. 1701 E. 17th Street

B. 1001 E. 17th Street

C. 821 Dunn Street

D. 800 Dunn Street

E. 901 E. 17th Street

Zora Clevenger was IU's first All-American in 1903. This photo was taken in 1901. (Indiana University Archives, P0020803)

9

WHO AM I?

You will have five hints to guess the name of each player. Points are awarded based on how quickly you can identify the person described. For example, you get 4 points if you guess the player on the first hint, 3 on the second hint and 2 on the third. You get 1 for either of the final two hints.

Player 1

1. I was named to six different All-American teams in 1944
2. I played center, but I called the offensive signals from there.
3. I also played defense and kicked extra points.
4. I was drafted in the fourth round of the NFL Draft, the 28th pick overall, by the Chicago Cardinals.
5. I was born in Newark, Ohio and I died in 1993 at the age of 72 in Johnstown, Ohio.

Player 2

1. I played linebacker on the 1967 Rose Bowl team and I was the first linebacker at IU to earn All-America honors.
2. I'm known for causing a fumble against Purdue late in the '67 game that assured our spot in the Rose Bowl.
3. I was inducted into the Indiana Football Hall of Fame in 2003.
4. I played high school football at South Bend St. Joseph where I played for Wally Moore.
5. I served as interim executive director of the Indiana Port Commission after I was appointed director in August, 2005, by Governor Mitch Daniels.

Player 3

1. Most people remember me for a field goal I kicked in the 2007 season.
2. It was from 49 yards out and helped us beat Purdue and go to a bowl game.
3. I'm from Logansport, Indiana and as a junior I made 21 of 23 field goals and earned second team All-American honors from the Associated Press.
4. I was also an Academic All-American at IU.
5. After IU, I went to Dental School at Ohio State University.

Player 4

1. I was a member of IU's first Big Ten team and earned All-America honors at center.
2. I served as athletic director at Missouri and Kansas State before taking that same position at IU.
3. I was IU's athletic director for 23 years.
4. In 1968 I became one of IU's six inductees into the College Football Hall of Fame.
5. Besides playing and coaching football, I was also the head basketball coach at IU from 1904-06.

Player 5

1. I was a first team All-American in 1963.
2. I was drafted in the first round by the Baltimore Colts, the eighth pick overall.
3. I was drafted as a defensive back, but I also led IU in rushing and receiving my junior season and I also was the top punt and kickoff returner, too.
4. I played a total of 72 professional games with both the Pittsburgh Steelers and New Orleans Saints.
5. I hail from Hattiesburg, Mississippi.

Player 6

1. I was a two-time All-American at Indiana playing linebacker on defense.
2. My senior season we beat both Ohio State and Michigan for the first time in history in the same year.
3. I'm from Coral Gables, Fla.
4. I was a third round selection of the Cleveland Browns in the 1988 NFL Draft.
5. I played five seasons professionally for both Cleveland and the Minnesota Vikings.

Player 7

1. In 1938 I was the first player selected overall in the National Football League Draft.
2. I was voted as the Big Ten's Most Valuable Player by the Chicago Tribune in 1937.
3. I played fullback.
4. I played four seasons with the Cleveland Browns before retiring in 1942.
5. I then served my country in World War II.

Player 8

1. When I left IU I was the top receiver in Indiana history and the first All-America pick in 20 years at that position.
2. I was a Biletnikoff Award finalist and set a new school record for receivers in 2007 with 16 TD grabs.
3. Terry Hoeppner was like a father figure to me.
4. I caught 36 touchdowns in my IU career was drafted.
5. I also played basketball at IU for Mike Davis.

Player 9

1. Many consider me one of the best running backs to ever play at Indiana.
2. Until Tevin Coleman came along and set the record a few years ago, I held the record for the most yards in a single season at 1,805.
3. I was sixth in the voting for the Heisman Trophy.
4. I only played two seasons at IU after transferring from Northeastern Oklahoma A&M
5. I was a first round draft pick of the New Orleans Saints in the 1992 NFL Draft and I hail from Fort Wayne, Indiana.

Player 10

1. In September of 1979, I led my team from a 26-3 halftime deficit against Iowa with 27 unanswered points in the second half to win 30-26.
2. I was also the quarterback that led my team to IU's first ever bowl victory.
3. I am one of only three IU quarterbacks, and at the time I was the second, to win Big Ten Most Valuable Player honors.
4. I was a two-sport athlete at IU and also lettered in baseball.
5. I was a 10th round draft pick of the Chicago Bears in the 1981 NFL Draft.

Player 11

1. I was recognized as a unanimous first team All-Big Ten selection my senior year and I was clearly the second best offensive player on my team.
2. My senior year I ran for 280 yards and six touchdowns in a win over Wisconsin.
3. I gained over 3,000 yards for my career.
4. Along my rushing yards, I also caught passes for more than 1,000 yards receiving in my career.
5. I played high school football at Evansville (Ind.) Bosses and was the Gatorade player of the year in the state after my junior season.

Player 12

1. I was a first team All-American as a wide receiver in 1969.
2. As a sophomore I played on the IU Rose Bowl team.
3. I caught 10 touchdown passes in my sophomore, junior and senior seasons.
4. I was a sixth round pick of the Atlanta Falcons in the 1970 NFL Draft.
5. I'm from Bloomington, Indiana.

Player 13

1. I'm the only Indiana University football player in the NFL Hall of Fame
2. I played in six Pro Bowls and three times led the NFL in receptions.
3. I played on the only outright Big Ten championship football team in IU history.
4. I earned first team All-American honors twice, once at end and once at fullback.
5. In between my playing stints at IU, I served a year in the U.S. Army in World War II.

Player 14

1. I'm a native of Kingston, Jamaica and I played high school football in Ontario, Canada.
2. I played for Bill Mallory at IU.
3. I started three seasons at right guard and was a second team All-American in 1994.
4. I was second round draft pick of the Miami Dolphins and also played with the Seattle Seahawks.
5. I played in the East-West Shrine Game and the Senior Bowl after my senior season.

Player 15

1. I was one of four Indiana All-American selections on the 1967 Rose Bowl team.
2. I was a team captain.
3. I started my career on the offensive side of the ball but switched to the defensive line before my senior year in 1967.
4. I had 76 tackles and three fumble recoveries my only season playing defense.
5. I was a first round pick of Miami in the 1968 NFL Draft.

Player 16

1. The Indiana football media guide says I'm considered to be one of the finest players to ever don an IU fooball jersey.
2. I was a first team All-American at fullback in 1964 and I had also had a 50-yard field goal that year against Ohio State.
3. As a junior in 1963, I led the Big Ten in rushing with 756 yards.
4. I was a first round draft pick, the 11th selection overall, by Detroit in the 1968 NFL Draft and I was a first round pick, the fourth pick overall, by the New York Jets in the 1968 AFL Draft.
5. I scored a touchdown for the Baltimore Colts in Super Bowl V.

Player 17

1. I hold the IU career record for touchdown passes in a career with 61.
2. I have a brother who played football at Brown, and another one who played at Nevada and is now an NFL tight end.
3. All four years at IU I completed at least 60 percent of my passes.
4. As a senior I threw for more than 3,500 yards and 27 touchdowns and led my team to a bowl game.
5. My junior season I injured my non-throwing shoulder and missed the final six games.

Player 18

1. When people think of Indiana University football most people think of me.
2. I was a two-time Big Ten rushing champion and led the nation in rushing and scoring my senior season.
3. I once ran for 377 yards in a game against Wisconsin.
4. I was enshrined in the College Football Hall of Fame in 2007.
5. I was an assistant coach at IU and now I'm an associate athletic director there.

Player 19

1. I was a second team All-American place-kicker.
2. I once held IU's single season record with 17 field goals.
3. As a senior, I connected on two 53-yard field goals and for my IU career I had six field goals over 50 yards.
4. My 58-yard field goal in a 1991 NFL Wildcard game is still the longest playoff field goal in NFL history.
5. I was drafted by the Miami Dolphins and made 272 field goals in a 12-year pro career.

Nate Sudfeld led Indiana to the 2015 Pinstripe Bowl in Yankee Stadium. (Indiana University Archives, 02_0830_md)

Player 20

1. I served as Indiana Governor Mitch Daniels' senior counsel and chief of staff during 2005 and 2006.
2. More people remember me as the quarterback on IU's only team to ever play in the Rose Bowl.
3. I was the MVP on the 1967 team that went to the Rose Bowl.
4. I was an academic All-American at Indiana.
5. I hail from Findlay, Ohio.

Player 21

1. I was a second team All American twice and a first team All American once at IU.
2. I played on IU's only outright Big Ten championship team.
3. I'm best known as the first African American player to be drafted by an NFL team.
4. I was a halfback, quarterback and punter.
5. I was drafted in the 13th round of the NFL Draft by the Chicago Bears and I went to the Pro Bowl with three different teams.

Player 22

1. I only played two seasons of football as a quarterback at IU but made my presence felt.
2. I threw six touchdown passes in one game my freshman year.
3. I was a first team All-American in 1943.
4. I played professional football for the Chicago Rockets, Brooklyn Dodgers, Chicago Hornets and Detroit Lions.
5. You might have a hunch about me.

Player 23

1. I was a two year starter at offensive tackle and played for Lee Corso.
2. I was a third team All American selection in 1977.
3. I was a junior college transfer from Garden City Junior College.
4. I was a 10th round selection of the Los Angeles Rams in 1978.
5. I hail from Springfield, Ohio.

Player 24

1. I was a Big Ten MVP at the quarterback position.
2. I was the first player in NCAA Division I history to pass for more than 40 touchdowns and score more than 40 touchdowns.
3. I threw for over 6,000 yards and ran for more than 3,000 yards in my career.
4. I also played basketball and baseball at IU.
5. As a receiver, I threw a touchdown pass in Super Bowl XL and have a Super Bowl ring.

Player 25

1. I had 10 interceptions in my IU career.
2. I was a third team All-American in 1996, which was Bill Mallory's final season at IU.
3. I played cornerback and safety at IU from 1994-96.
4. I hail from Indianapolis.
5. My senior year I had five interceptions, 67 tackles and three fumble recoveries.

Player 26

1. As a senior at IU I had 66 catches for 1,265 yards and 13 touchdowns.
2. I earned first team All-American status that season.
3. We went to a bowl game by junior season but not my senior year at IU.
4. I was known for having great hands and for excellent acceleration both in and out of routes.
5. I'm from Elkhart, Indiana.

Player 27

1. I was the quarterback when we won the first outright Big Ten championship.
2. The next season, my senior year, I was a second team All-American.
3. I was a 26th round draft pick of Philadelphia in the 1947 NFL Draft.
4. I played for the All-American Football Conference's New York Yankees.
5. I started at William & Mary before coming to IU.

Player 28

1. I was a third team All-American at end at IU but I'm known more for being a doctor.
2. I was the IU team physician for the 1967 Rose Bowl team.
3. I was IU's first Academic All-American.
4. I won the Balfour Award for bringing honor and distinction to IU.
5. I'm in the Indiana Football Hall of Fame and the Indiana Athletics Hall of Fame.

Player 29

1. I'm one of only three IU football players to earn first team All-American honors in two different seasons.
2. I led the 1967 Rose Bowl team in rushing.
3. I broke the 1,000 yard rushing barrier for the first time in a season as a senior in 1969
4. I was a second round draft pick of San Francisco in the 1970 NFL Draft.
5. Some people remember me as the player fans would chant "Punt, John, Punt" at because I had a propensity for running with the ball out of punt formation.

Player 30

1. As a senior at IU, I had 199 tackles including 142 solo stops.
2. That broke a school record that had been 165 tackles before.
3. I was a second team All-American at IU in 1978.
4. I had 444 tackles for my career and also have the school record for tackles in a game with 26 against Ohio State.
5. I was a second round pick of Seattle in 1979.

Player 31

1. I am IU's school record holder for interceptions in a season and a career.
2. I had a 62-yard punt return for a touchdown in the 1979 Holiday Bowl.
3. I had a 98-yard interception return for a touchdown against Michigan State in 1978.
4. I was a second team All-American in 1980.
5. I attended Ben Davis High School in Indianapolis and I'm a member of the Indiana Football Hall of Fame.

Player 32

1. I am the only player in IU history to have returned a punt, interception and fumble for a touchdown.
2. I was a co-captain on the 2007 IU team that played 13 in honor of Terry Hoeppner.
3. I had 16 career interceptions, which is second all time.
4. I returned a Peyton Manning pass that I intercepted in the Super Bowl for a touchdown.
5. I was drafted in the second round of the NFL Draft by the New Orleans Saints and I've played for five NFL teams.

Player 33

1. I'm one of two two-time Academic All-Americans at IU
2. I also had five interceptions and let my team in tackles as a senior in 2006.
3. I had 278 total tackles in my career.
4. I hail from Chesterfield, Missouri.
5. I was named the Big Ten's freshman defensive player of the year by the Sporting News.

Player 34

1. I was Indiana's second football All-American selection.
2. I was a second team All American in 1928.
3. I played professional football until 1936.
4. I played a total of seven seasons for the Chicago Cardinals, the Portsmouth Spartans, and the Detroit Lions.
5. I was born in Chicago and I died in 1972 at the age of 65 in Glendale, California.

Player 35

1. Like many others on these pages, I played on the outright Big Ten championship team in 1945.
2. I was a first team All-American at the end position on that team.
3. I was a 17th round pick of the Chicago Cardinals in the 1947 NFL Draft.
4. I was also an assistant football coach at IU in 1950 and 1951.
5. In high school in Kentucky, I was a two-time state champion in the pole vault and held the state record in that event.

Player 36

1. In my junior season in 2014, I rushed for 307 yards against Rutgers, the second most yards in school history in a game.
2. I hold the IU school record for rushing yards in a season with 2,036.
3. I was one of three finalists for the Doak Walker Award and I was seventh in the Heisman Trophy voting.
4. I was drafted by the Atlanta Falcons in the third round of the 2015 NFL Draft.
5. I'm from Tinley Park, Illinois.

Player 37

1. I am IU's career record holder in sacks and tackles for loss.
2. My best year was my sophomore year when I had 10 sacks and 21 tackles for loss.
3. I played my first year for Bill Mallory and my final three seasons for Cam Cameron.
4. I played 11 seasons in the NFL after being signed initially by the Miami Dolphins as an undrafted free agent in 2000.
5. I'm from Nigeria but I played my high school football in Staten Island, New York.

Player 38

1. I played quarterback at IU and then play in the NFL for 15 seasons.
2. Since retiring from the NFL, I have done work on both radio and television, most recently with CBS Sports.
3. I led the 1991 Hoosiers to a Copper Bowl victory.
4. In my last two college bowl games, I ran for five touchdowns.
5. I made a large donation to IU that was used to provide a new locker room for the football team at Memorial Stadium.

Player 39

1. When I left IU I was second all-time in career points behind Anthony Thompson.
2. I had 320 career points and no season with less than 69.
3. I had 53 career field goals made and at least nine made field goals in every season.
4. I had strings of 10, 9 and 8 consecutive field goals at different times in my career.
5. My career long field goal was 50 against Michigan in 2013.

Player 40

1. When I left IU I was in third in all-purpose yards with 4,658.
2. In 2006 I had three kickoff returns for touchdowns including returns of 100 and 98 yards.
3. As a freshman I had 432 receiving yards and my last three seasons I never had less than 387 rushing yards.
4. I was known by my teammates as being one of the best-dressed players on the team.
5. I've played on seven different NFL teams after originally being signed as an undrafted free agent by Philadelphia.

Player 41

1. I rushed for more than 3,300 yards in my four-year at IU.
2. My best season was my freshman year in 1976 when I ran for 1,028 yards.
3. My dad was a backfield mate of Hopalong Cassady on Ohio State's 1954 national championship team.
4. My brother, Rob, played fullback at IU two years behind me.
5. When I left IU I was the career rushing leader and was a fifth year senior after sitting out 1977 with a broken leg.

Player 42

1. Not an IU player but I'm the only Indiana coach who has been inducted into the College Football Hall of Fame.
2. I coached at IU for 14 seasons from 1934-47 and had a record of 63-48-11.
3. I coached IU's only outright Big Ten title team in 1945.
4. My playing career was at Centre College in Kentucky.
5. Following the 1945 season, I was the national coach of the year.

Player 43

1. I had 16 100-yard games at Indiana.
2. My best game was 245 yards against Purdue in the Old Oaken Bucket game in 1994.
3. I had 1,475 yards that season for the Hoosiers.
4. I had two years over 1,200 yards rushing and finished my career with 3,492 yards and 21 touchdowns.
5. I was Mr. Football in the state of Indiana from Franklin County in 1992.

Player 44

1. I rushed for 2,781 yards in my first three seasons at Indiana.
2. My senior year, however, I was injured and only gained 8 yards.
3. I rushed for 211 yards against Purdue in 1975.
4. I had 11 100-yard rushing games in my IU career.
5. The week before the Purdue game in 1975, I ran for 194 against Wisconsin.

Player 45

1. I was a high school phenom at Sheridan (Ind.) High School in terms of running the ball.
2. My junior season alone I had 66 touchdowns in high school and I shattered multiple national records.
3. I had 250 college football scholarship offers but chose to stay close to home at Indiana.
4. My top game at IU was 240 yards in 1992 against Missouri.
5. Unfortunately, I only had one other rushing game over 100 yards in college.

Player 46

1. I won a Super Bowl ring as a receiver with the Denver Broncos in the 2016 Super Bowl.
2. I had 2,042 yards and 17 touchdowns in three seasons at IU.
3. I had seven 100-yard receiving games at IU with a top performance of 189 yards versus Illinois in 2013.
4. I was second round pick of the Denver Broncos in the 2014 NFL Draft.
5. I hail from Dayton, Ohio, Jefferson Township.

Player 47

1. I had nine 300-yard passing games at Indiana.
2. My career best was 480 yards passing against Michigan in 2010.
3. I threw for 7,251 yards in my career with 45 touchdowns.
4. I also had games of 366 and 382 yard.
5. I played high school football in Bloomington, Indiana.

Player 48

1. Not an IU player but I coached Indiana to more bowl appearances than any other IU coach.
2. I coached IU for 13 seasons and had a record of 69-77-3.
3. I also coached at Miami (Ohio), Colorado and Northern Illinois.
4. I am one of only seven coaches to coach three different programs to top 20 national finishes.
5. In 1987 I became the first Big Ten coach ever to earn back-to-back coach of the year honors.

Player 49

1. I was the quarterback on the 2007 team that played in the Insight Bowl.
2. I had 17 games of 200 yards passing or more and four of better than 300 yards.
3. My best game was 354 yards against Ball State in 2007.
4. I had 6,395 yards for my IU career and 48 touchdowns.
5. I played my senior season at Valdosta State.

Player 50

1. Not an IU player, but I was the head coach at Indiana for two seasons.
2. Two traditions I brought to IU included 'The Rock' and 'The Walk'
3. My time at IU was cut short when I died of brain cancer in June of 2007.
4. Later that season my team accomplished my goal of playing 13 games and made it to the Insight Bowl in Tempe, Arizona.
5. My favorite poem was 'Never Quit' which is something I'm forever remembered by at IU.

George Taliaferro was one of IU's most talented players ever and one of its biggest ambassadors later in life. (P0027177)

10

THE ANSWERS

Chapter 1 — The Warm Up

1. C. 1
2. B. 1960
3. A. Rose Bowl
4. C. Holiday Bowl
5. B. 1945
6. C. Bo McMillin
7. A. 1
8. B. 1891
9. C. 1925
10. E. 1940's
11. D. 1950's
12. B. Michigan State
13. A. Kentucky
14. A. Anthony Thompson
15. B. Tevin Coleman
16. C.Antwaan Randle El
17. C. 3
18. C. 10
19. B. 1994

20. E. Marcus Thigpen
21. A. Anthony Thompson
22. B. 2
23. D. 5
24. B. 1
25. E. 1
26. B. 4
27. B & E. Bill Mallory and John Pont
28. C. San Diego, Calif.
29. D. Birmingham, Ala.
30. E. Memphis, Tenn.
31. C. Peach Bowl
32. D. Copper Bowl
33. D. Shreveport, La.
34. B. Tempe, Ariz.
35. Yankee Stadium
36. B. False
37. A. True
38. A. True
39. E. IU has never beaten Penn State in State College
40. E. 0-4
41. E. 1
42. E. 2
43. E. 5
44. B. 10
45. B. 5
46. D. 6

47. A. True
48. A. True
49. B. False
50. D. Xavier

Chapter 2 — Player Trivia

1. B. Vern Huffman
2. B. 3
3. A. True
4. D. Antwaan Randle El
5. A. James Hardy
6. C. 5
7. D. Ben Chappell
8. A. Antwaan Randle El
9. B. Kellen Lewis
10. A. Anthony Thompson
11. E. 52
12. D. Jay Rodgers
13. B. He moved him to wide receiver
14. E. One game
15. D. North Carolina State
16. C. Tommy Jones
17. D. Ben Chappell
18. A. True
19. B. Nate Sudfeld
20. E. 2015
21. D. 6
22. C. Jason Spear

23. A. Griffin Oakes
24. D. Joe Norman
25. E. 26
26. A. Adewale Ogunleye
27. C. Tim Wilbur
28. B. Mike Dumas
29. B. Devine Redding
30. C. & D. Will Meyers and John Hammerstein
31. E. George Taliaferro
32. A. Anthony Thompson
33. C. Tim Clifford
34. A. & D. Ben Chappell and Nate Sudfeld
35. C. Tim Wilbur
36. B. Simmie Cobbs Jr.
37. B. Kellen Lewis
38. D. Trent Green
39. A. Vaughn Dunbar
40. D. Trent Green
41. D. Mark Hagan
42. C. Damon Watts
43. B. Mike Dumas
44. A. Thomas Lewis
45. C. John Paci
46. D. Austin Starr
47. C. Tim Jorden
48. B. Van Waiters
49. C. Dave Schnell
50. C. Ernie Jone

Chapter 3 — Coaching Trivia

1. D. 2
2. A. Bill Mallory
3. B. Bo McMillin
4. D. 8
5. B. Louisville Athletic Club
6. B. Clyde Smith
7. D. Louisville
8. D. 1
9. B. Billy Hayes
10. B. John Pont
11. B. Don't Quit
12. E. Bo McMillin
13. E. All of the above
14. C. Bill Lynch
15. B. 5
16. B. 10
17. A. Bernie Crimmins
18. C. 9
19. C. Bob Hicks
20. A. Wyoming
21. D. Tennessee
22. C. Sam Wyche
23. A. Terry Hoeppner
24. B. Sam Wyche
25. C. 2
26. E. 3
27. D. Louisville

28. E. 6
29. C. 2
30. C. 8
31. A. 0
32. C. 3
33. B. 5
34. B. Virginia Tech
35. D. Terry Hoeppner
36. B. Lee Corso
37. B. A.B. Woodford
38. E. Cam Cameron
39. C. Cam Cameron
40. D. 2
41. A. Rick Greenspan
42. C. Miami
43. C. Ben Roethlisberger
44. C. December, 2005
45. B. Southern Illinois
46. E. All of the above
47. E. Bill Lynch
48. D. Insight
49. A. 1
50. C. Buck Suhr

Chapter 4 — Fun Facts Trivia

1. D. He was an assistant football coach at IU
2. A. One year. (Actually just a few months)
3. C. Bo Van Belt

4. B. They didn't allow a touchdown the entire season
5. B. No. They finished 6-1, losing to Illinois 3-0.
6. C. 1988. Played in the Peach Bowl on Jan. 2, 1988 and the Liberty Bowl on Dec. 28, 1988.
7. C. Three. Two bowl games and Kentucky in 2001 when it was rescheduled because of 9/11.
8. C. Isaiah Roundtree. He was actually a pretty good basketball player but never played at IU.
9. D. He never played in a bowl game.
10. B. John Harbaugh
11. C. He won a bronze medal in the hammer throw in the Olympics in Stockholm
12. B. First Downs
13. E. 114
14. A. Bob Hoernschemeyer
15. B. Ernie Jones
16. A. John Isenbarger
17. C. Courtney Snyder
18. B. Babe Laufenberg
19. A. Nate Lundy
20. C. Van Waiters
21. C. Matt Lovecchio
22. D. Mark Deal
23. A. True
24. B. False
25. B. & D. The Rock and the Walk
26. B. Some of the limestone used to build Memorial Stadium

27. C. At Gentry Farm

28. D. Miami

29. B. Ted Kluszewski

30. D. Taking batting practice for the IU baseball team

31. A. He threw six touchdown passes in one game

32. A. True. They played in 1991 in South Bend with the Irish winning 49-27.

33. E. Baseball

34. E. Franklin

35. C. Dunn Cemetery

36. B. Turned it into an ice skating rink

37. A. True. It was documented by a janitor in that building

38. E. IU defeated both Michigan and Ohio State in the same season.

39. A. True

40. B. 7

41. B. 7

42. D. No. 4

43. C. Two hours

44. D. $2.50

45. D. Three. The most recent time was the 2001 season when the Kentucky game was moved to early December because of 9/11.

46. B. 1942

47. A. True. In 1945, IU was No. 4 and Purdue was No. 18 when they met.

48. A. True.

49. A. True. IU was 0-7-1 in history before beating

Louisville Athletic Club 30-0 in the final game of the 1891 season.

50. B. False. False. Fisch is old but he's not that old.

Chapter 5 — Hoosiers in the Pros Trivia

1. C. 12
2. D. 7
3. A. True
4. A. Vern Huffman
5. D. Arizona
6. A. True
7. A. True
8. B. False
9. B. Second
10. B. Second
11. E. Eighth
12. B. Second
13. E. Not drafted
14. E. Eighth
15. B. Fifth
16. B. Second
17. D. Sixth
18. B. Second
19. B. Second
20. E. 26th
21. B. Washington
22. C. Seattle
23. E. San Diego

24. A. St. Louis

25. A. Philadelphia

26. C. Denver

27. D. Miami

28. B. Baltimore

29. A. New York Giants

30. A. Jacksonville

31. A. One

32. B. St. Louis

33. A. Pittsburgh

34. C. Philadelphia

35. C. Cam Cameron

36. D. Pete Pihos

37. B. George Taliaferro

38. B. Oakland

39. D. Minnesota

40. E. Cleveland

41. B. Baltimore Ravens

42. B. Tracy Porter

43. A. Rodger Saffold

44. C. Marv Woodson

45. D. Atlanta

46. B. John Isenbarger

47. B. Ben Raimondi

48. D. Bob Hoernschemeyer

49. D. Adewale Ogunleye

50. E. Rex

Chapter 6 — 1967 Football Trivia

1. C. 3
2. A. 1-8-1
3. C. 8
4. D. 10
5. D. 4
6. D. 1950
7. C. Minnesota
8. B. No. 4
9. D. No. 3
10. E. The Hoosiers were not ranked
11. A. Doug Crusan
12. E. 13
13. A. 2
14. D. 30
15. D. 1954
16. B. 1950 vs. Notre Dame
17. E. 6
18. A. 1
19. D. O.J. Simpson
20. C. The Cardiac Kids
21. A. True
22. A. No. 1
23. A. No. 1
24. D. 1
25. B. 4
26. C. Jade Butcher

27. D. 3
28. A. Terry Cole
29. C. Harry Gonso
30. B. John Isenbarger
31. E. 2
32. B. False
33. E. 3
34. D. 1
35. E. 0
36. A. True
37. A. True
38. A. True
39. B. False
40. B. False
41. B. False
42. C. Most receiving touchdowns in a season
43. C. Jade Butcher
44. B. False. He was actually the first to earn All-American honors at linebacker in school history.
45. B. False. Pete Pihos did it, too.
46. C. Findlay
47. A. Harry Gonso
48. C. Tom Bilunas
49. B. Brown. As in Brown Marks
50. Three. Center Harold Mauro, QB Harry Gonso and DT Harold Dunn.

Chapter 7 — Venue Trivia

1. B. University Athletic Field at IU's Seminary Square
2. A. 1885
3. A. David Starr Jordan. The field was also named for its proximity to the Jordan River.
4. E. Rose Polytechnic. In 1971, the school's name was changed to Rose Hulman Institute of Technology.
5. C. 8,000
6. E. The parking lot next to the IU Memorial Union
7. A. True. It was placed there on Oct. 11, 1980.
8. E. 1915
9. C. The country was preparing to go to war. In the spring of 1916, the country was preparing to go to World War I.
10. A. & D. A new women's dormitory and an auditorium that could also be in the form of a Student Union.
11. E. $400,000
12. E. The current site of the Fine Arts Museum. The artist's rendering placed the stadium east of Wildermuth Fieldhouse on the current site of the Fine Arts Museum
13. E. What is now an area that stretches from Woodlawn Avenue to Jordan Avenue. It was north of the Men's Gymnasium on the area now known as Woodlawn Field
14. B. Bedford Steel and Construction
15. B. A concrete issue. On June 20, the entire structure was condemned because it had been determined that the concrete possessed only 80

percent of the strength it should have had to be safe

16. B. Indiana Field. Indiana Field had been used as a practice facility. The field is now beneath the current Ora. L. Wildermuth Fieldhouse.
17. A. True. Although only 3,000 students and townsfolk arrived, forcing the film director to adjust his camera angles
18. B. Washington Park
19. C. Trains. The Indianapolis Southern Railroad announced that two trains would run from Bloomington to Indianapolis and back the day of the game
20. C. Wabash
21. A. True
22. A. $256,487.09
23. C. 22,000. It the later years 21,742 could sit in the concrete section, 2,052 in the three-tier stands on the west side and 7,606 in the steel bleachers on the northeast side of the stadium that were added in the late 1940s. The total was more than 31,000.)
24. E. A DVD of the construction progress for the stadium
25. B. False
26. E. 23,000 yards
27. A. On 10th Street where the Arboretum now stands
28. C. The debut of the Old Oaken Bucket
29. A. The first Little 500 race
30. E. 7,000
31. A. Bill Armstrong Stadium
32. D. 1960

33. D. Aug. 27, 1958
34. D. $4.56 million
35. B. Oregon State
36. D. Marquette
37. B. 48,454
38. D. 52,929
39. E. Purdue
40. A. Ohio State
41. E. All of the above
42. B. 10th Street Stadium
43. B. 1982
44. B. Indiana won all of its home games
45. E. 1969
46. B. Grass
47. A. True
48. A. True. In technical terms, the heavy rains washed away the gravel substrate and created a large sink hole
49. B. 2007
50. B. In time for the 2018 season

Chapter 8 — Who Wore that Number?

1. A. 32
2. B. 11
3. D. Allen Webb
4. C. 6
5. C. 26
6. E. 14
7. D. 44

8. D. 5
9. E. 18
10. B. False
11. A. True
12. B. False
13. B. False
14. A. True
15. B. False
16. A. True
17. A. 48
18. A. True
19. D. 82
20. B. False
21. B. 46
22. B. 2
23. C. 38
24. E. 42
25. D. 51
26. A. 77
27. C. 83
28. E. 0
29. B. 93
30. B. 61
31. B. 78
32. B. 33
33. C. Matt Bomba
34. E. 81

35. E. 19
36. C. 64
37. C. 3
38. C. 2
39. B. 2
40. A. Smith
41. C. Johnson
42. B. 2
43. E. 15
44. E. 12
45. A. 1
46. B. 1
47. C. 4
48. E. 7
49. E. 30
50. B. 1001 E. 17th Street

Chapter 9 — Who am I?

1. John Tavener
2. Ken Kaczmarek
3. Austin Starr
4. Zora Clevenger
5. Marv Woodson
6. Van Waiters
7. Corby Davis
8. James Hardy
9. Vaughn Dunbar
10. Tim Clifford

11. Levron Williams
12. Jade Butcher
13. Pete Pihos
14. Andrew Greene
15. Doug Crusan
16. Tom Nowatzke
17. Nate Sudfeld
18. Anthony Thompson
19. Pete Stoyanovich
20. Harry Gonso
21. George Taliaferro
22. Bob Hoernschemeyer
23. Charlie Peal
24. Antwaan Randle El
25. Mike Dumas
26. Ernie Jones
27. Bob Raimondi
28. Brad Bomba
29. John Isenbarger
30. Joe Norman
31. Tim Wilbur
32. Tracy Porter
33. Will Meyers
34. Clare Randolph
35. Bob Ravensburg
36. Tevin Coleman
37. Adewale Ogunleye

38. Trent Green
39. Mitch Ewald
40. Marcus Thigpen
41. Mike Harkrader
42. Bo McMillin
43. Alex Smith
44. Courtney Snyder
45. Brett Law
46. Cody Latimer
47. Ben Chappell
48. Bill Mallory
49. Kellen Lewis
50. Terry Hoeppner